AF291707

The

Southern Way

The regular volume for the Southern devotee

Peter Waller

Issue 73

www.crecy.co.uk

© 2026 Crécy Publishing Ltd
and the various contributors

ISBN 978-1-80035-364-0

First published in 2026 by Crécy Publishing Ltd

Contact details
All editorial submissions to:
The Southern Way
Crécy Publishing Limited
1a Ringway Trading Estate
Shadowmoss Road
Manchester M22 5LL
enquiries@crecy.co.uk

All rights reserved. No part of this book may be reproduced or transmitted in any form or by any means electronic or mechanical, including photocopying, recording or by any information storage without permission from the Publisher in writing. All enquiries should be directed to the Publisher.

A CIP record for this book is available from the British Library

Publisher's note: Every effort has been made to identify and correctly attribute photographic credits. Any error that may have occurred is entirely unintentional.

Printed in the UK by ESP Colour

Crécy Publishing Limited
1a Ringway Trading Estate
Shadowmoss Road
Manchester M22 5LH

www.crecy.co.uk

Front cover:
6 May 1961 No 73119 *Elaine* is seen passing through Clapham Junction at speed; see the article on BR Standard Class 5s on the Southern on page 20.
Les Folkard/Online Transport Archive

Back cover:
Three Class 207 DEMUs survived into the 21st century; for a brief period in the early 1990s all were reduced to two-car sets but reverted to three-car formations in May 1995. Here, on 13 January 2002, one of this trio – No 207203 – is seen at Hastings having just arrived from Ashford. This was the last of the type to remain operational, being withdrawn in January 2005.
Henry Pryer/Online Transport Archive

Title page:
The current rolling stock in use on the Ashford to Hastings line are Class 171 DMUs. Here, on 5 April 2018, No 171722 is seen at Lewes with the 10.32 service from Brighton to Ashford International. See the article on the history of the line starting on page 5. *Alex Dasi-Sutton*

Contents

Issue No 74 of THE SOUTHERN WAY
ISBN 978-1-80035-363-3
available in August 2026 at £14.95

To receive your copy the moment it is released, order in advance from your usual supplier, or it can be sent post-free (UK) direct from the publisher:

Crécy Publishing Ltd

1a Ringway Trading Estate, Shadowmoss Road, Manchester M22 5LH

Tel 0161 499 0024

www.crecy.co.uk

enquiries@crecy.co.uk

Introduction

There is a very well-known cliché: 'Familiarity breeds contempt'. This was brought strikingly home to me a month or so ago when I ventured through Waterloo station heading to and from Woking. Something was missing: for the first time in the 40 or so years that I have been regularly passing through the station I did not see a single Class 455 unit.

For more than two decades when I was living in the Staines area, the '455s' were an almost daily sight. Sometimes in use for getting to and from work; sometimes viewed from the offices at Shepperton as they plied their trade on the branch services. And because they were so familiar I recorded them relatively infrequently; they were on the doorstep and, somehow, they would always be there. I would travel widely and record scenes in faraway places but I largely ignored what was around me at home. I grew up in Bradford, not far from the trolleybus depot on Duckworth Lane; however, the only photographs I ever took of the structure was when it was almost too late: preliminary demolition work had just commenced.

Of course, when the depot was being demolished and when I first got to know the Class 455s at Waterloo station physical film was expensive – particularly if you were still at school or just starting out on a professional career – and so its use was sparing. Again, the familiar was ignored because there would always be another occasion to see it.

As time has progressed and digital photography has arrived so the excuse of cost is no longer as valid as it used to be. Modern phones produce images that are capable of reproduction in books and magazines; indeed, even stills from video recorded on a mobile can still provide a workmanlike image if required. Without the constraint of cost, there is really no excuse for not recording the present as, in the future, you may look back and regret not recording those everyday scenes that were once so much part of your life.

Peter Waller

On 22 August 1983, less than six months after the Class 455s were introduced to passenger service, No 5801 is pictured at Waterloo. This unit was one of the class that ended up in operation with the South Central franchise and was finally withdrawn in May 2022.
Geoffrey Tribe/Online Transport Archive

The Ashford-Hastings Line

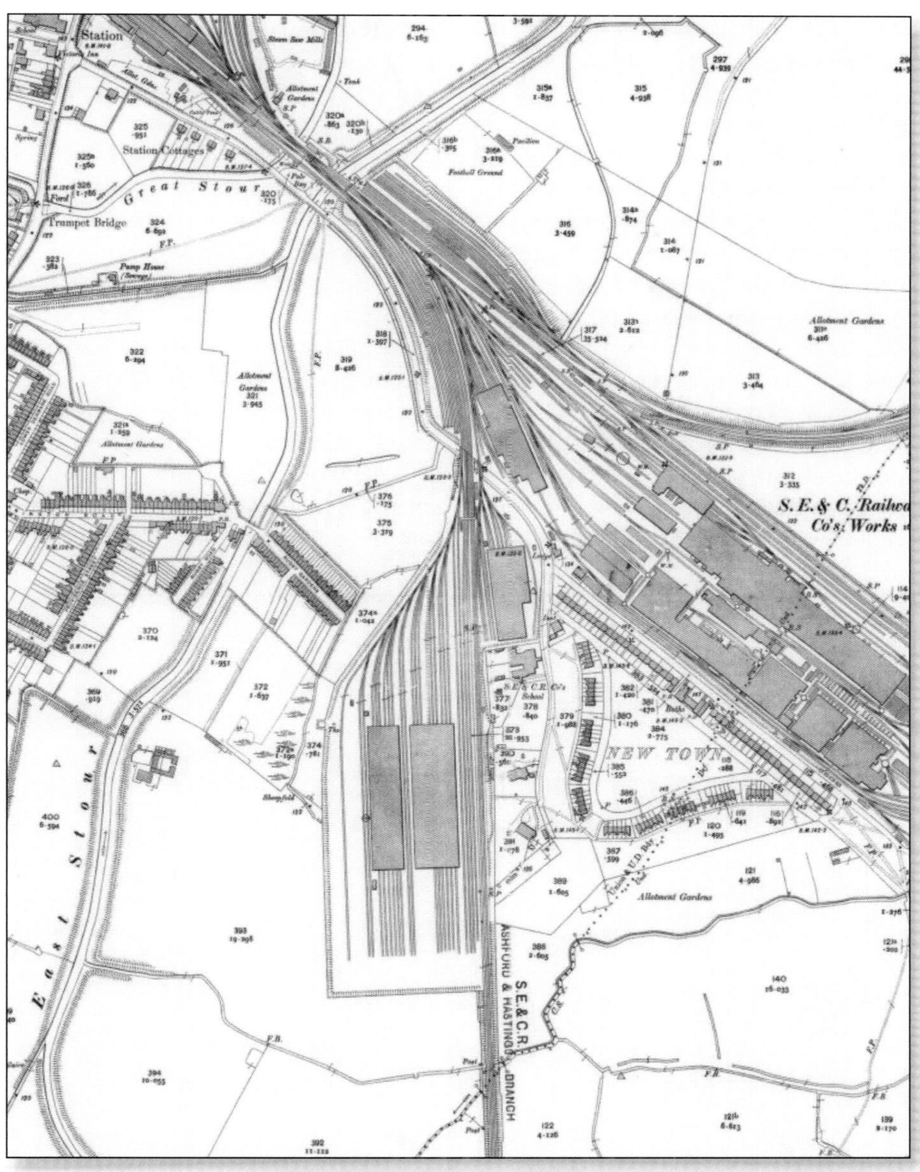

The line to Hastings heads southwards from Ashford turning off the main line just to the east of the station. This 1907 map shows clearly the junction and the extensive facilities that the SECR had built for its workshops in the town.
Reproduced with the permission of the National Library of Scotland

There were relatively few lines in Kent that were either threatened with closure or actually closed as a result of the Beeching report of 1963. Although a number of lines were subject to modification, the only line actually to close was the branch to New Romney whilst the section from Ashford to Hastings was listed for closure but reprieved. The 175th anniversary of the opening of the latter occurred on 13 February 2026.

Backing by the London & Brighton Railway was authorised on 29 July 1844 to construct the 32½-mile line along the south coast (although construction was actually in the hands of the independent Brighton, Lewes & Hastings Railway; this was not formally absorbed into the L&BR until 27 July 1846, shortly after the first sections of the route were completed, when the larger company was renamed the London, Brighton & South Coast). The line opened from Brighton to Lewes on 8 June 1846, thence to Bulverhythe on 27 June 1846, to St Leonards on 7 November 1846 and, finally, to Hastings on 13 February 1851.

The route of the new line took the L&BR into territory that the South Eastern Railway had been looking to exploit; indeed, it had its own plans for the extension of the line from Hastings to Ashford. Contemporaneously with the proposals for the BL&HR, the SER had sought to promote its own line from Headcorn to Hastings via Rye but the Board of Trade's support for the BL&HR saw the SER switch its attention to the construction of a line from Hastings to Ashford via Rye. Construction of this line was authorised, with construction initially in the hands of the BL&HR subject to the SER assuming operation of the line if it wished. In the event, the BH&LR handed over the construction to the SER. However, although the route was perceived as having strategic importance (with certain obligations imposed on the SER as a result), there was little progress on construction initially as the two competing railways had differing views over the best route; the LBSCR maintained its preference for the original alignment via Ore and Rye whilst the SER preferred a cheaper route via Whatlington. Although some construction work commenced in 1847, it was not until the following year that the route was finalised and construction seriously commenced. Initially, work saw the line constructed for single track but, during construction, the decision was made to double the track throughout.

Although it had originally been hoped that the line would open in October 1850 and then on 1 January 1851, additional delays meant that it was not until 13 February 1851 that services actually commenced. When the line opened, there were four intermediate stations – Ham Street (known as Ham Street & Orlestone from 1 February 1897 to 3 May 1976), Appledore (with the suffix 'Kent' from 12 May 1980), Rye and Winchelsea. Winchelsea station was, however, initially short-lived as it closed on 1 September 1851; reopened the following year – probably on 1 January – it carried the suffix 'Halt' from 12 September 1961 until 5 May 1969. Additional stations opened at Ore on 1 January 1888, at Three Oaks Halt on 1 July 1907 – this station was renamed Three Oaks & Guestling Halt in 1908 and the 'Halt' suffix was dropped on 5 May 1969 – and at Doleham Halt again on 1 July 1907 (this too lost its suffix in May 1969).

Inevitably there was tension between the two railways; for a period, the SER blocked access to Hastings station to services operated by the LBSCR and it took a court action before matters were resolved provisionally; it was not until an agreement on 5 December 1870 that a final deal was struck in which SER services were permitted to terminate at St Leonards Warrior Square.

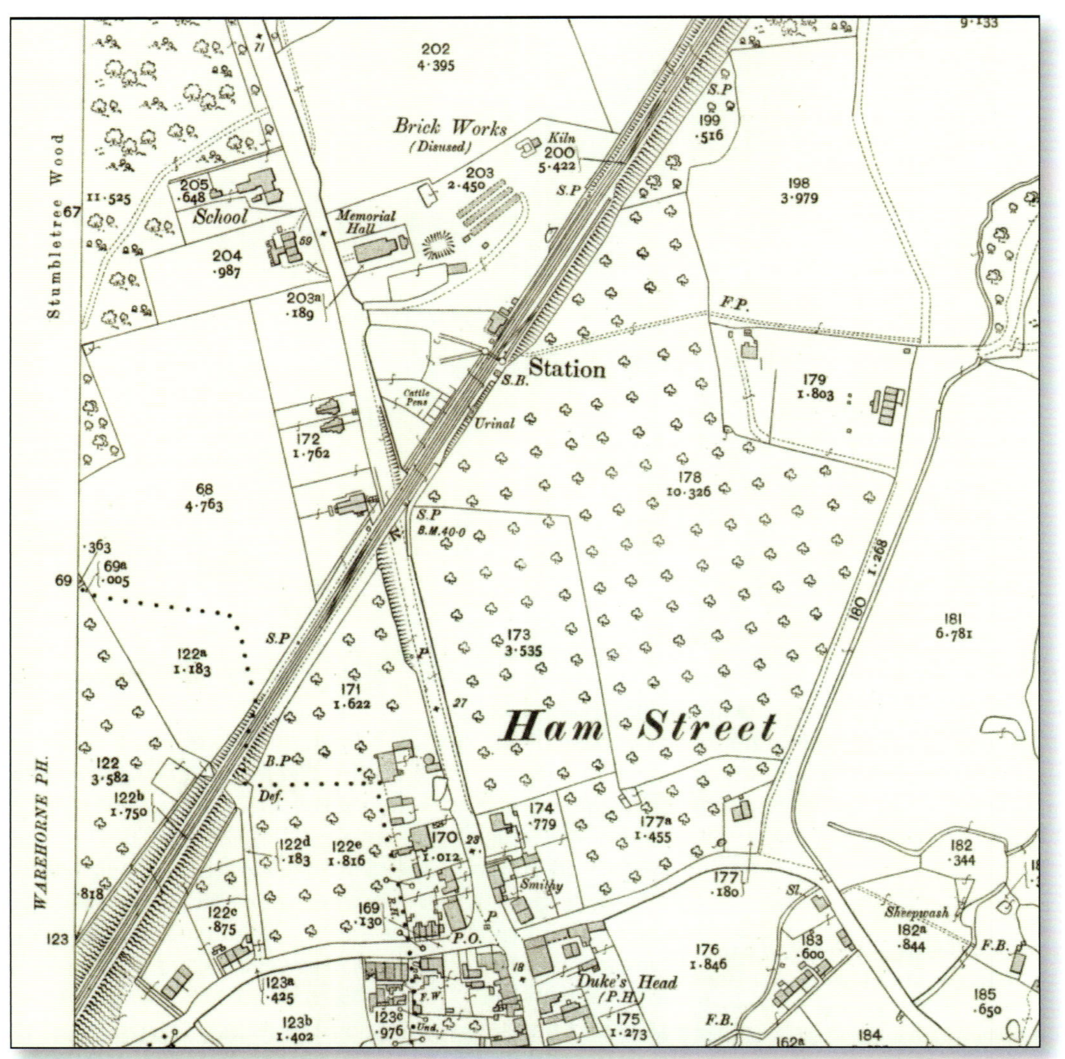

The first intermediate station to be encountered heading southwards is Ham Street, as recorded in 1907. The station had been renamed Ham Street & Orlestone on 1 February 1897; it was not to revert to simply Ham Street until 3 May 1976.
Reproduced with the permission of the National Library of Scotland

In March 1854 a short branch – less than half-a-mile in length – opened from Rye to serve the local harbour; this had originally been proposed some eight years earlier. A more significant branch was that constructed eastwards from a junction at Appledore. The SER had plans – never fulfilled – to create and build a facility at Dungeness for use by cross-Channel steamer services. On 30 July 1866, Royal Assent was granted to the South Eastern Railway Act 1866; the powers granted included the construction of a branch to Denge Beach on Romney Marsh. These powers were modified by a further Act, which received the Royal Assent on 5 August 1873 to permit the line's extension to Dungeness and the construction of a new 100-yard pier. However, work on the line did not progress and a new company – the Lydd Railway – was incorporated on 8 April 1881, when the Lydd Railway Act 1881 received the Royal Assent, to construct the line from Appledore to Dungeness. The new railway was promoted by Robert William Perks with the contractor being Thomas Andrew Walker. The line opened throughout to Dungeness for freight traffic on 7 December 1881 but passenger services initially operated only as far as Lydd; the latter were extended to Dungeness on 1 April 1883. By this date a three-mile extension to New Romney & Littlestone ('on-Sea' was added in 1888) had been authorised – on 24 July 1882 – and this was opened on 19 June 1884. The Lydd Railway retained its independence until it was absorbed by the SER on 20 September 1895.

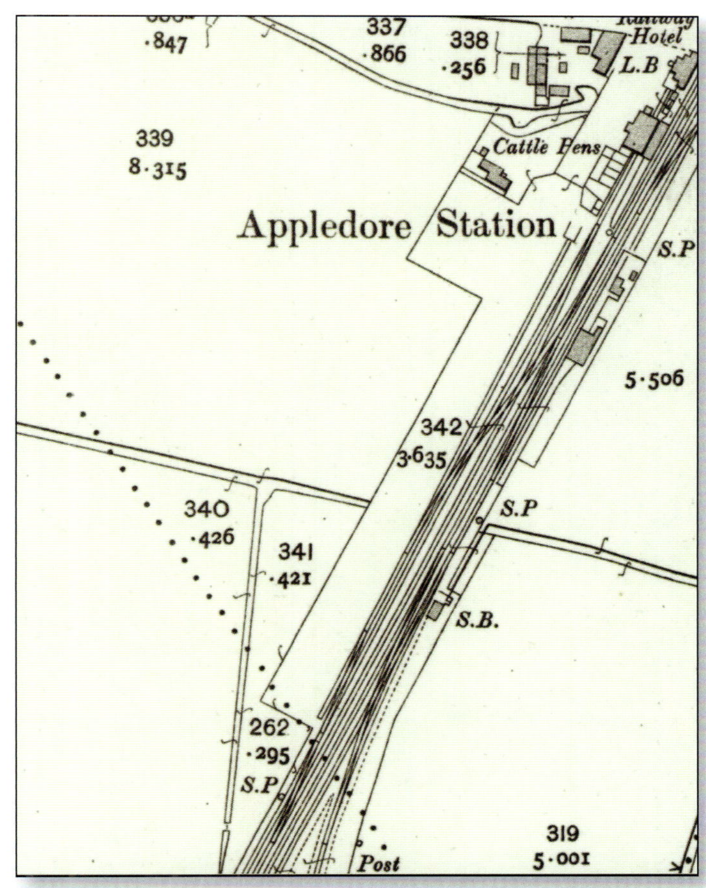

Above right: **Of all the stations on the line, Appledore was the most inconveniently located to the population it purported to serve, being some 1½ miles from Appledore itself. The station became the junction for the line to Dungeness on 7 December 1881 with the opening of the independent Lydd Railway's branch.**
Reproduced with the permission of the National Library of Scotland

Right: **Rye station in 1909; the branch to serve Rye harbour – just under half-a-mile in length – was opened in March 1854. It can be seen heading south-eastwards from the main line at the bottom left of the map.**
Reproduced with the permission of the National Library of Scotland

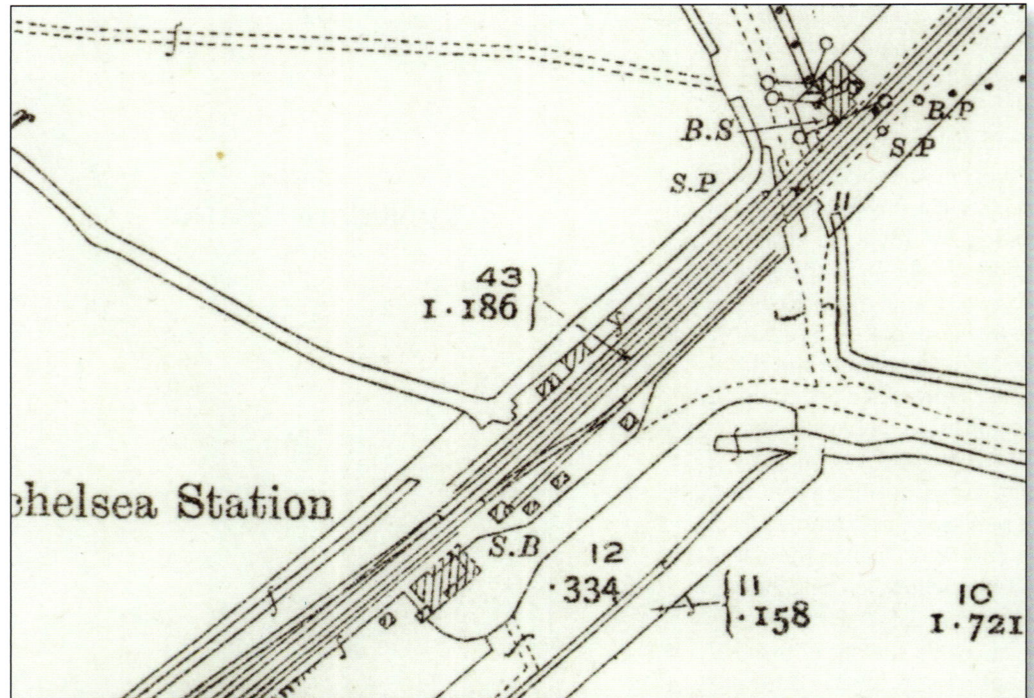

Winchelsea in 1929; the station carried the suffix 'Halt' from 12 September 1961 until 5 May 1969.
Reproduced with the permission of the National Library of Scotland

The only closed station on the line is Snailham Halt; when recorded here in 1909, the station was only two years old, having opened as Snailham Crossing Halt on 1 July 1907. It was renamed Snailham Halt by August 1909. The halt, which was situated about half-a-mile from the nearest houses and accessed via an unsurfaced country lane, was never modernised and closed on 2 February 1959.
Reproduced with the permission of the National Library of Scotland

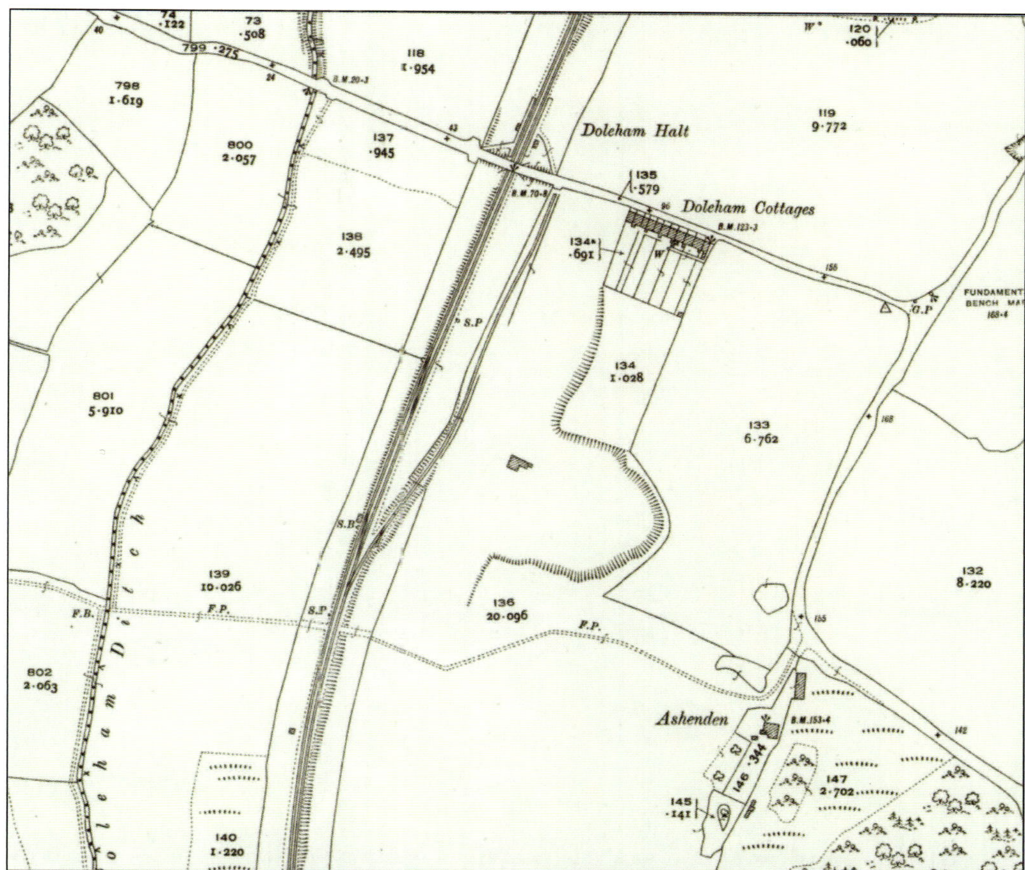

Known as Guestling Halt when first opened on 1 July 1907, the station was renamed Doleham Halt the following year. The two-platform station is recorded here in 1929. The single siding, situated to the south of the station, was closed on 6 February 1961.
Reproduced with the permission of the National Library of Scotland

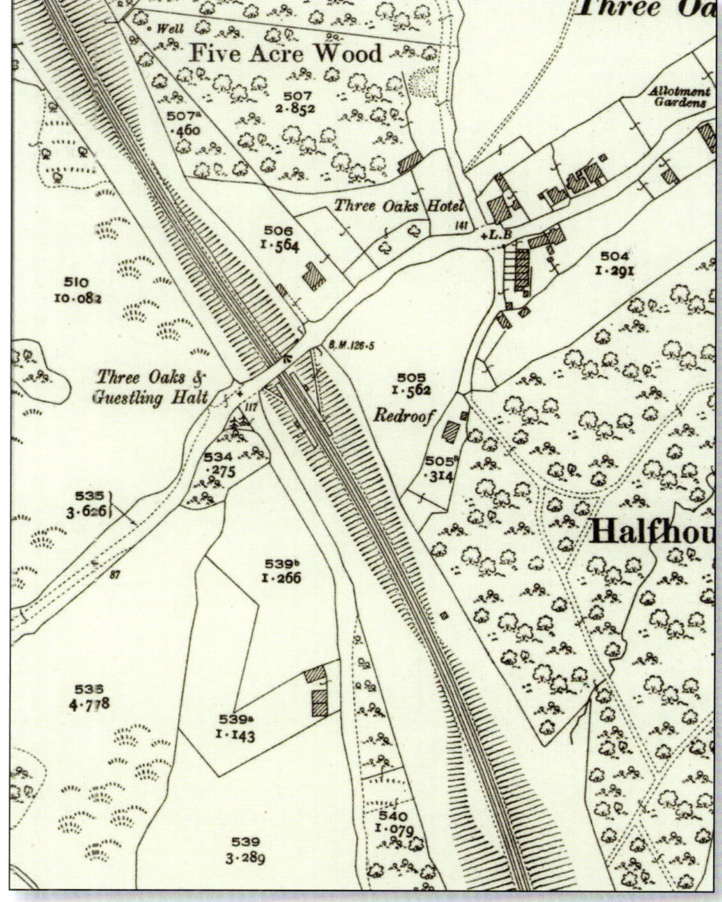

Three Oaks & Guestling Halt, seen here in 1929, was opened on 1 July 1907 as Three Oaks Halt; '& Guestling' was added early the following year. The station was renamed simply as Three Oaks on 5 May 1969.
Reproduced with the permission of the National Library of Scotland

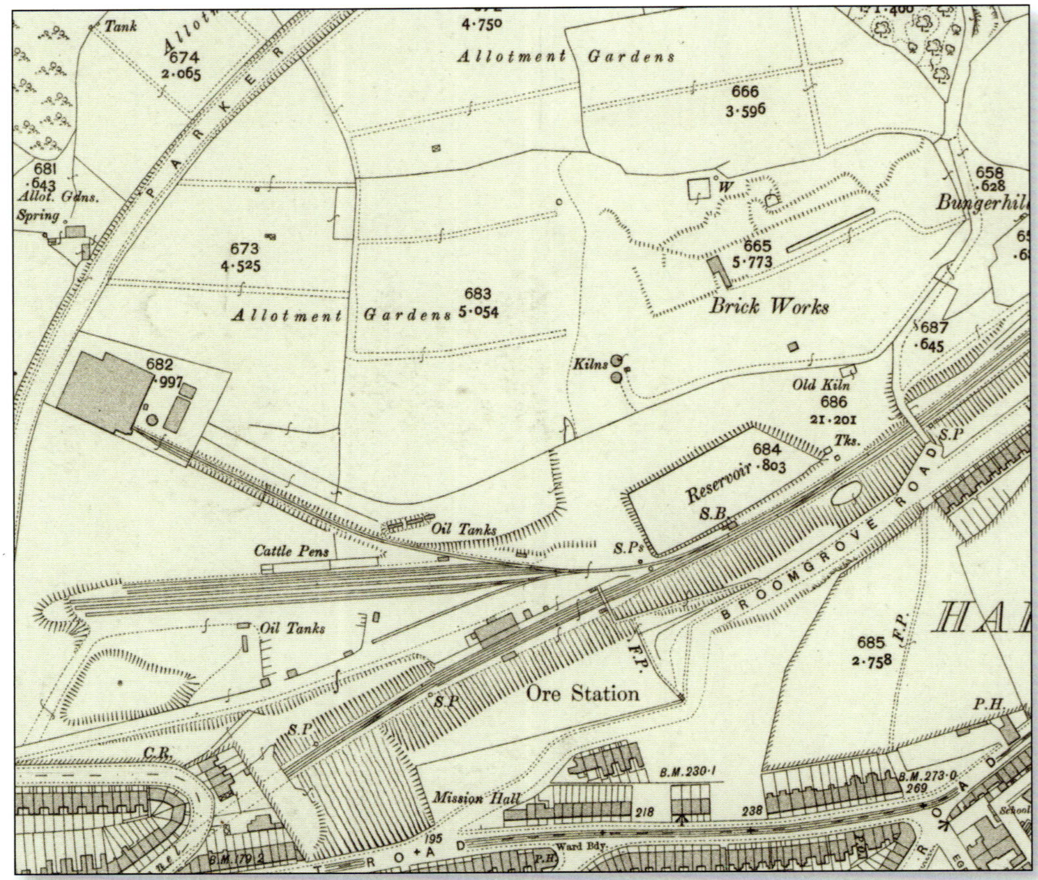

The station at Ore opened on 1 January 1888; this map records the station in 1909. The section from Hastings to Ore was electrified from 7 July 1935; this is the only stretch of the line through to Ashford that has been so treated. Public freight facilities were withdrawn from Ore on 1 May 1973.
Reproduced with the permission of the National Library of Scotland

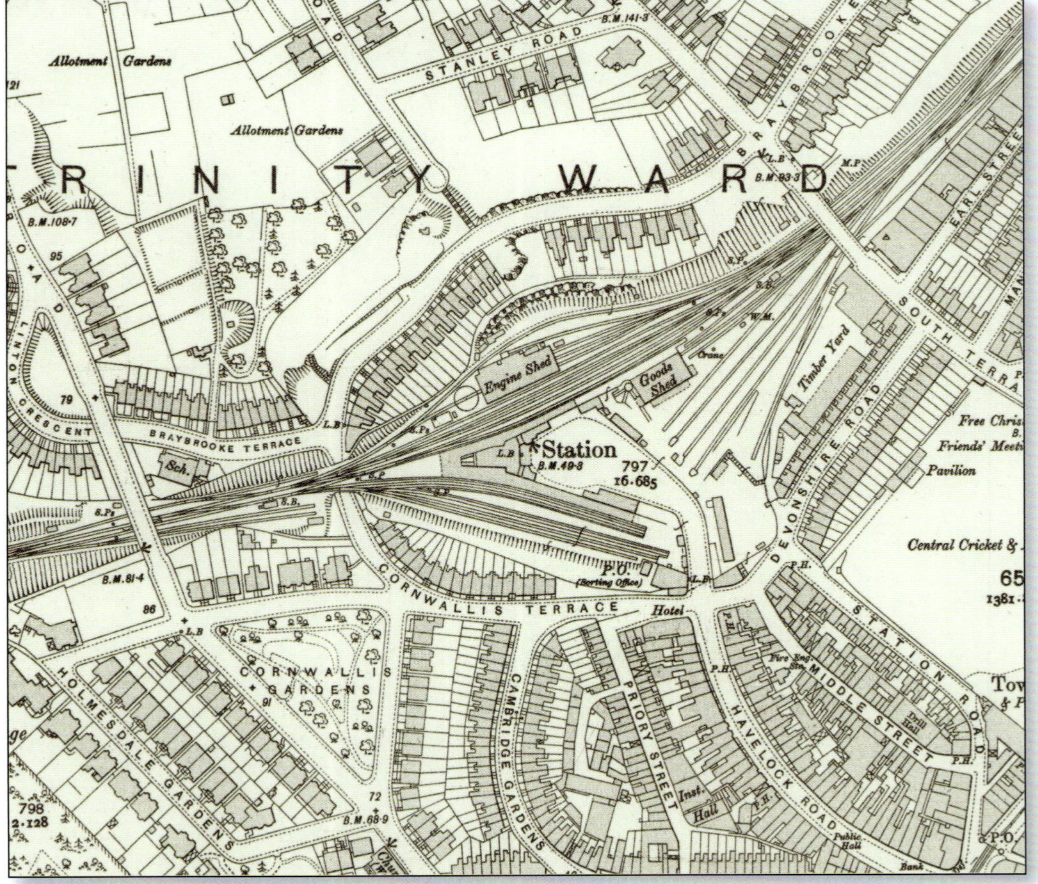

Hastings station and its environs as they existed in 1910. The engine shed that was situated on the north side of the station site was closed in 1929 in order to facilitate the rebuilding of the station; this work was completed in 1931 with the new station designed by James Robb Scott in a neo-Georgian style. The station was further rebuilt in 2006. Freight facilities were withdrawn from Hastings on 3 May 1971.
Reproduced with the permission of the National Library of Scotland

Opposite top: **The timetable for the Ashford-Hastings line plus that for the New Romney branch for April 1910.**

Bottom: **The timetable for the service in August 1939.**

LONDON, ASHFORD, LYDD, NEW ROMNEY, DUNGENESS, and HASTINGS.—South Eastern and Chatham.

Down.

Miles from Ashford	Station	Week Days																Sundays					
		mrn	mrn	mrn	mrn	mrn	aft	aft	aft	aft	aft	aft	aft					mrn	mrn	aft		aft	aft
	228 Charing Cross ....dep.			5 15		8 25	11 0		12 7		4 25	5 25	7 10					7 50	10 2			7 7	
	228 Waterloo Junc. „			5 17		8 27		12 9				5 33	7 20	Fridays only.				7 52	10 4			7 9	
	228 Cannon Street „			5 25		8 38	11 5		1215		4 33	5 33	7 20					8 0	1010			7 17	
	228 London Bridge „			5 32		8 45	1112		1222			5 37	7 25					8 9	1014			7 24	
5¼	Ashford ....dep.	7 10		8 27		1045	1 0		3 45	6 0		7 15	9 16					8 10	1055	3 45	7	9 20	
8¼	Ham St. and Orlestone..	7 19		8 35		1053	1 8		3 53	6 9		7 23	9 25					8 18	1110	3 53	7 14	9 28	
	Appledore	7 25		8 43		11 0	1 15		4 1	6 18		7 30	9 34					8 24	1110	3 59	7 20	9 34	
11	Appledore ....dep.	7 27	7 37		9 50	11 8	1 24		4 25	6 25	7 37	b 3 8	8 37	9 k 40				8 25		4 0		7 32	
15¼	Brookland	7 32	7 42		9 55	1113	1 29		4 30	6 30	7 42	b 8 18	8 42	9 k 45				8 30		4 7		7 37	
	Lydd ....arr.	7 42	7 52		10 5	1123	1 39		4 40	6 40	7 52	b 8 18	8 52	9 k 52				8 40		4 15		7 47	
19¼	Lydd ....dep.	7 43		8 30	10 7	1125	1 41	3 54	4 41	6 42	7 53	8 20	8 53		Tuesdays only.			8 41		4 45		7 48	
	*New Romney ..arr.	7 52		8 39	1016	1134	1 50	3 14	4 50	6 51	8 2	8 29	9 2	10 k 5				8 50		4 54		7 57	
19¼	Lydd ....dep.		7 53			1155	2 25		5 25			8 55						9 10		4 16			
	Dungeness ....arr.		8 2		m 12 4	m 2 34		m 5 34			9 8 4							9 19		4 25			
15¼	Rye			8 55	1050	1114	1240	28 3		4 16	5 0	6 30	7 45	9 48	1150			1123	4 20		7 32	9 47	
17¼	Winchelsea ¶¶			9 5	1055	1119	1245	1 343	10	4 21	5 6	6 36	7 51	9 54				1130	4 24		7 39	9 53	
23¼	Ore			9 15	1124	1134	1 14	49 3	39	4 40	5 34	6 54	8 8	1012				1145	4 45		7 54	1014	
26¼	Hastings 180, 241 .. arr.			9 22	1130	1138	1 20	53 3	45	4 45	5 40	7 0	8 13	1017	1210			1150	4 50		8 0	1019	

Up.

Mls	Station	mrn	a mrn	mrn	mrn	mrn	aft	aft	m aft	aft	aft	aft	aft	aft	aft	aft	aft	mrn	mrn	aft	aft	aft
	Hastings ....dep.	6 45	8 9	9 55	1155	1235	2 15	3 40	3 55	5 35	6 10	7 16						1115	6 50	1230	2 50	5 45
3	Ore ¶¶	6 49	8 14	9 10 0	12 0	1239	2 20	3 44	4 0	5 39		7 22						1119	6 54	1234	2 54	5 49
9	Winchelsea	7 4	8 9	1027	1227	1254	2 47	4 0	4 7	5 54		7 42						1134	7 9	1249	3 15	6 10
11	Rye	7 11	8 9	9 30	1033	1233	1 0	2 53	4 6	4 36	6 2	8 7	7 42					1139	7 14	1254	3 20	6 15
	Mls Dungeness......dep.		8 10	8 10			1220		2 45		5 40								9 24		4 30		
4	Lydd (above).....arr.		8 19	8 19			1229		2 54		5 49								9 33		4 39		
	*New Romney ..dep.	6 45	8 20	9 10		1030	1237	2 5	3 30		5 5		7 58	6 8	3 59		9 6	1015		8 56		5 5	5 5
	Lydd (above)...arr.	6 54	8 29	9 19		1039	1246	2 14	3 39		5 14		7 14	8 18	4 49	9 15		1024		9 5		5 14	5 12
8½	Lydd ....dep.	6 56	8 30	9 21		1041	1250		3 41		5 51	7 15	8 18		9 10	9 18	9 18			9 34		5 15	5 13
11	Brookland		9 9	9 31		1051	1 0		3 51		6 1	7 25	8 27		9 44					9 44		5 25	5 23
	Appledore ....arr.	7 12	8 42	9 36		1056	1 5		3 56		6 6	7 30	8 32		9 20	9 29	9 30			9 49		5 30	5 28
17¼	Appledore (see above)	7 26	8 43	9 46			1 15		4 21		6 15	6 41	7 55				9 31			7 28	9 50	1 7	5 31
20¼	Ham St. and Orlestone..	7 33	8 48	9 54			1 22		4 29		6 21		8 4							7 35	9 55	1 15	5 36
26¼	Ashford 228, 231 ...arr.	7 45	8 57	10 5			1 33		4 40		6 32	6 55	8 15		9 44					7 46	10 5	1 26	5 45
80¼	231 London Bridge.. arr.	1011		1135			3 43		7 20			1016								9 46			7 10
81	231 Cannon Street.. „	1015	1034	1140			3 48		7 25			1021								9 52			9 10
81½	231 Waterloo Junc. „	1021	1041	1147					7 32			1031								9 59			9 19
82¼	231 Charing Cross.. „	1025	1045	1151					7 36			1035								10 4			7 18

a Littlestone-on-Sea Fast Train.   **b** Except Fridays.   **c** By slip carriage.   **k** Wednesdays and Fridays.
m Steam Car, one class only, calling at the Halts.   **s** Saturdays only.
¶ New Romney and Littlestone-on-Sea.   ¶¶ "Halts" at Snailham, Doleham, and Three Oaks and Guestling, between Winchelsea and Ore.

ASH and ALDERSHOT TOWN (South Camp).—South Eastern and Chatham.

Down.

Miles	Station	Week Days																							
		mrn	mrn	mrn	mrn	mrn	mrn	aft	aft	aft		aft	aft	aft	aft	aft	aft	aft	aft		aft	aft	aft	aft	ngt.
	Ash ....dep.	8 48	8 35	9 5	9 42	1052	1142	1253	1 16	2 6	Sats.	2 e 43	3 6	3 55	4 35	5 11	5 40	6 e 32	6 38	Sats.	7 e 29	7 44	Sats.	8 46 9 39	1032 11 5 12 6
3	Aldershot Town (S.C.) arr.	8 10	8 41	9 11	9 48	1058	1148	1259	1 22	2 6		2 e 10	3 12	4 1	4 41	5 17	5 46	6 e 38	6 44		7 e 35	7 50		8 52 9 45	1038 1111 1212

Up.

Miles	Station	Week Days																					
		mrn	mrn	mrn	mrn	mrn	mrn	aft	aft	aft	aft	aft	aft	aft	aft	aft	aft	aft		aft	aft	aft	aft
	South Camp, Aldershot Town .....dep.	7 30	8 20	8 50	9 27	1032	1113	1230	1 4	1 40	2 50	3 38	4 18	4 52	5 25	6 6	7 e 7	7 11	Sats.	8 31	9 20	1016 1045	1120
3	Ash 248, 249 ......arr.	7 36	8 26	8 56	9 33	1038	1119	1236	1 10	1 46	2 56	3 44	4 24	4 58	5 31	6 12	7 e 13	7 17		8 37	9 26	1022 1051	1126

Station	Sundays										Station	Sundays									
	mrn	mrn	aft	aft	aft	aft	aft	aft	aft	aft		mrn	mrn	mrn	aft	aft	aft	aft	aft	aft	aft
Ash ....dep.	7 10	9 5	9 45	1242	4 50	5 30	7 55	1015	1052	1133	South Camp, Aldershot Town ...dep.	6 52	8 50	9 30	1228	1254	5 14	7 28	9 55	1035	11 5
Aldershot Town (S.C.) ..arr.	7 16	9 11	9 51	1248	4 56	5 36	8 1	1021	1058	1139	Ash 248, 249 ......arr.	6 58	8 56	9 36	1234	1 0	5 20	7 34	10 1	1041	1111

e Except Saturdays.

LONDON, ASHFORD, LYDD TOWN, NEW ROMNEY, RYE, and ORE.

Down.

Miles from Ashford	Station	Week Days																							
		mrn	mrn		mrn	mrn	mrn		mrn	mrn	mrn	mrn	mrn		mrn		noon		aft	aft	aft	aft	aft	aft	aft
	322 Charing Cross dep.				7 11				9 15		1015		11 5		11 15		12 0		1 15	1 15		2 15	2 25	3 15	3 15
	322 Waterloo ..... „				7 13				9 17		1017		11 7		11 17				1 17	1 17		2 27		3 17	3 17
	322 Cannon Street „				7 11														1 2	1 2		1438	1534		
	322 London Bridge „		3 y 45		7 23				9 18	9 18			11 18				12 18	12 18			1141	2034		2 34	2 34
	322 Victoria ..... „		3 y 0		7 18									11 18			12 k 48		1 18	1 18		2 18	2 18		
	Ashford (Kent) ....dep.	5 40	8 0		9 10		9 42		9 55	1048		1133	11 55	12 55		1 12		1 30		2 35		2 52		3 42	4 10
5½	Ham Street & Orlestone..	5 48	8 8				9 50			1056			1 8	1 20											4 48
8½	Appledore	5 54	8 13				9 57		10 7	11 3		1144		1 8		1 26		1 42		1 54	2 46		3 3	3 53	4 27
11	Appledore ....dep.	5 56	8 26				9 59			1111		1145		1 9				1 43			2 47			3 54	
15½	Brookland	6 3	8 26				10 5			1118				1 15				1 49			2 53			4 0	
16½	Lydd Town	6 13	8 35				10 14			1127				1 24				1 59			3 2			4 9	
18½	Lydd-on-Sea H	6 41	8 42				10 20			1135		12 6		1 31				2 6			3 10			4 15	
20½	Greatstone-on-Sea	6 46	8 47				10 25			1140		1212		1 36				2 13			3 17			4 20	
22	New Romney L ....arr.	6 51	8 52				10 30			1145		1217		1 41				2 18			3 22			4 27	
15½	Rye		8 25		9 31	9 50			1018	1114	1137		12 16			1 39				2 5		3 14	4 10		4 38
17½	Winchelsea		8 30			9 56				1141			12 20							2 10		3 19	4 14		4 42
19½	Snailham Halt					10 0				1147										2 16			4 20		
21½	Doleham Halt ..[Halt		8 38			10 5				1152										2 21			4 24		
22½	Three Oaks & Guestling		8 42			1010				1157										2 26		3 24	4 29		
25½	Ore		8 48			1016				12 4										2 33		3 31	4 36		5 36
26½	Hastings 232, 343 arr.		8 52		9 49	1020			1036	1131	12 8		12 36			1 56				2 37		3 v 35	4 40	4 59	5 40

Down. Week Days—Continued / Sundays

Station	aft	aft	aft	aft	aft	aft	aft	mrn	mrn	mrn	mrn	mrn	mrn	mrn	aft	aft	aft	aft	aft	aft	aft	aft	aft	aft
322 Charing Cross dep	4 S 0 34		5 31	6 15			7 34		7 15				1215		3 15									8 15
322 Waterloo „	4 S 0 36		5 33	6 17			7 36		7 17				1217		3 17									8 17
322 Cannon Street „	5 S X 0		6 18						7 24															8 23
322 London Bridge „	4 S 0 43	4 S X 42	5 45	5 34			7 45		7 24				9 20	1018										
322 Victoria „	4 S 0 18	1 L 52	5 20	5 18	5 Y 53	7 2			7 18	8 20							5 18	5 18						
Ashford (Kent) ....dep.	6 10	6 54	7 40	7 45	8 59	9 42	7 58		9 40		1030		1150	1252	1 10		2 15		4 55		7 13	7 13		9 45
Ham Street & Orlestone..	6 18					9 50	8 6		9 48		1038		1158								7 21	7 21		9 53
Appledore	6 25	7 6	7 52	7 57		9 56	8 12		9 54		1044			12 4			2 27		5 7		7 27	7 27		9 59
Appledore ....dep.	6 32		8 4	8 4		10 6	8 12				1044						2 27		5 7	5 55		7 40		
Brookland	6 38		8 10	8 10		10 12	8 18				1050						2 33		5 13	6 0		7 46		
Lydd Town	6 47		8 19	8 19		10 24	8 30				11 2				1 16		2 45		5 26	6 9		7 54		
Lydd-on-Sea H	6 55		8 27	8 27		10 31	8 38				1110				1 24		2 53		5 38	6 16		8 1		
Greatstone-on-Sea	7 0		8 32	8 32		10 36	8 43				1115						2 58		5 43	6 21		8 7		
New Romney L ....arr.	7 4		8 37	8 37		10 41	8 47				1119				1 35		3 2		5 49	6 26		8 14		
Rye	6 20	6 37	7 17	8 4	8 9		9 11	9 39	10 6	11		1125		1216	1250	31 2 20	3 20	5 0		6 39	7 39			1012
Winchelsea	6 24		8 9	8 14			10 16		9 43			1129		1221	1254	2 24	3 24	5 4		6 43	7 45		9 14	1017
Snailham Halt	6 30		8 15	8 20								1134			1259	2 29	3 29	5 9		6 48			9 19	
Doleham Halt ...[Halt	6 35		8 20	8 25					9 52			1138				2 33	3 33	5 13		6 52			9 23	
Three Oaks & Guestling	6 40		8 25	8 30					9 57			1143				2 38	3 38	5 18		6 57			9 28	
Ore	6 48		7 32	8 31	8 36		10 32		10 5			1151	1236		1 16	2 46	3 46	5 26		7 5	8 3		9 36	1032
Hastings 232, 343 arr.	6 52		7 36	8 35	8 40	9 36	10 37		1010	1026		1156	1240		1 21	1 50	251	3 51	5 30		7 10	8 7	9 41	1037

H For Dungeness.   **H** Arr Greatstone 7 10 and New Romney 7 15 aft Wed. and Thurs.   **L** New Romney and Littlestone-on-Sea.   **k** 10 mins. later on Sats.
L Dep. 4 18 aft on Sats.   **n** 5 mins. earlier on Sats.   **S O** or **S0** Saturdays only.   **S X** or **SX** Saturdays excepted.   **V** 15 mins. earlier on Sats.
v 3 mins. later on Sats.   **Y** Dep. 6 18 aft. on Sats.   **y** 3rd class only.   **+** Not after 4th Sept.   **‡** Change at London Bridge.

For OTHER TRAINS between Ore and Hastings, see page 232

Pictured at Lydd Town, where there was a passing loop on the otherwise single-track branch, with the 1.52pm service from New Romney to Ashford on 10 November 1966 is Class 205 No 1118. *John A. M. Vaughan*

Opposite top: **On 20 March 1987 Class 203 DEMU No 203001 is seen awaiting departure from Ashford platform 1 with the 10.44 service to Hastings.** *Dennis C. Ovenden*

Bottom: **Ham Street & Orlestone (as the station was called at the time), like a number of other stations on the line, has staggered platforms and on 27 July 1982 Class 206 No 1206 is pictured with the 15.47 service from Hastings to Ashford. The Italianate style of the station building is typical of the architecture of the line's structures.** *Brian Morrison*

When recorded, the signal box at Appledore was a relatively recent structure; a Southern Railway Type 16 box and equipped with a 37-lever frame, it opened on 27 June 1956. It replaced an earlier box that had been situated between the western end of the Hastings-bound platform and the junction to New Romney; the new structure also included a gate wheel, thus rendering the gatekeeper redundant. The line south from Appledore to Rye was singled on 30 September 1979. Prior to the box's closure, the level crossing was converted to an automatic open crossing without barriers; the latter were subsequently added. The box closed on 6 November 1995, with control now in the hands of the Ashford Integrated Electronic Control Centre, and was subsequently demolished. *Geoffrey Tribe/Online Transport Archive*

Opposite top: **In March 1964 a DEMU heads westbound towards Hastings. The junction of the New Romney line can be identified in the distance. Passenger branches over the branch ceased on 6 March 1967.** *Phil Tatt/Online Transport Archive*

Bottom: **On 19 June 1958, Class H 0-4-4T No 31276 stands in the platform at New Romney & Littlestone-on-Sea station. The coaching stock comprises push-pull set No 650; this was formed of two non-corridor coaches: Third No S2087S (Diagram No 64) and Brake Composite No S6940S (Diagram No 437). The former was built by Brown Marshalls to a design of Billinton in 1895; it was reframed for push-pull use in November 1930. The latter was built at Lancing to a design of Marsh in June 1921. The set was withdrawn in September 1959.** *B. K. B. Green*

Following the withdrawal of passenger services to New Romney, the branch was retained to serve the nuclear power stations constructed at Dungeness. In August 1985 No 73003 is pictured shunting nuclear flasks at the CEGB siding at Dungeness. The two nearest flasks have been discharged while the three beyond the locomotive are full with one being loaded. Both of the power stations, now owned by EDF, have been closed but decommissioning work is expected to take many decades. *A. A. J. Procter*

On 1 January 1888 an additional station – Ore – opened to the east of Mount Pleasant Tunnel. The original station in Hastings was poorly sited to serve many of the residential areas to the east of the town centre. This was not resolved until 1886 when a landowner offered the SER £1,000 towards the cost of the new station. When built, the railway crossed the River Rother to the east of Rye over a swing bridge; from the early 1880s onwards it was proposed that this be replaced by a fixed structure, although it was not until 1903 that the work was completed.

In order to improve the finances of the line, the SECR – which had been created through the creation of a joint committee of the South Eastern and London, Chatham & Dover railways – introduced a steam railmotor service between Ashford and Hastings. Three new halts were opened on 1 July 1907 for the new service: Guestling (renamed Doleham in 1908), Snailham and Three Oaks ('& Guestling' added in 1908). Although Snailham Halt closed on 2 February 1959, the other two remain open, having dropped the 'Halt' suffix on 5 May 1969. The steam railmotor service survived until 1920.

Post-grouping, the Southern's electrification work saw the third rail extended to Hastings; in order to provide a servicing facility for the new EMUs away from Hastings station, the third rail was extended through to Ore and a new facility was established on the north side of the station to accommodate and maintain the stock. As a result electric services operated through to Ore station. With the electrification of the line south through Tunbridge Wells to Hastings in May 1986 and the use of St Leonards for EMU maintenance, the shed at Ore was closed and subsequently demolished.

The branch line to New Romney was modified in the 1930s. On 4 July 1937, the line was altered so that it now ran – closer to the coast and to the Romney, Hythe & Dymchurch Railway – from a point just east of Lydd station to serve new stations at Lydd-on-Sea (suffixed 'Halt' from 14 June 1954) and Greatstone-on-Sea (also redesignated 'Halt' from 14 June 1954). The revision also resulted in the closure on 4 July 1937 to passenger services to Dungeness. This section, however, retained a freight service until early 1952.

Never a great success financially, the line and the New Romney branch were inevitably, perhaps, to become threatened by the Beeching report in March 1963, with both slated for closure. The branch did succumb, with closure being approved on 23 February 1966 by the then Minister of Transport, Barbara Castle, and being carried out on 6 March 1967. As far as the Ashford-Ore line – the section from Hastings to Ore was not threatened – was concerned there was considerable opposition. As a short term measure to save money, the line was temporarily operated as a single track between Appleford and Ore between June 1965 and September 1966. On 1 April 1966 John Morris was appointed Parliamentary Under Secretary of State for the Ministry of Transport; he commented on 5 May 1967 that the line remained under review but would not close without further advice.

Over the next decade the future of the line remained in doubt. In 1969 it was reported that the line would be closed by the end of the year; this proved an inaccurate forecast. Following the Conservative Party's electoral win in 1970, Michael Heseltine was appointed to the role that John Morris had held between 1966 and 1968. His boss, John Peyton, as Minister of Transport, was not made a member of the cabinet as the role had been reduced to non-cabinet rank when Fred Mulley replaced Barbara Castle in 1969. On 26 November 1970,

In order to reduce operating costs, the section south from Appledore to Ore was singled with a passing loop retained at Rye. On 11 August 1984 Class 201 No 1004 is seen departing from Rye with the 13.40 service from Hastings to Ashford. *R. S. Freeman*

Heseltine announced that the line would only be closed when there were improvements made to the bus service between Ashford and Ore. In 1971 both the *Kent Messenger* and *The Times* confidently stated that withdrawal of passenger services would be achieved by the end of the year. Two years later, on 5 December 1973, Peyton, by this time Secretary of State for the Environment, which oversaw transport, announced that the line's future was again under discussion with the local authorities and on 31 July 1974 it was reported that the ministry would recommend the line's closure but that services would be maintained for the foreseeable future. In order to save money, the line was singled between Ore and Appledore on 1 October 1979, with a passing loop retained at Rye. Further savings have been effected by the reduction in line speed and other changes.

The branch to Dungeness was retained post-closure to New Romney in order to serve the nuclear power stations at Dungeness. Over the years two complexes have been operational at the site. Dungeness A – a Magnox station – opened in 1965 with Dungeness B – the first Advanced Gas-cooled Reactor in Britain – following in 1983; the former closed on 31 December 2006 with the latter being taken out of service in 2021 prematurely. Both are currently undergoing decommissioning – work that will probably take towards the end of the current century before it is completed. At one stage, there was a possibility that one of the new generation of nuclear power stations – designated Dungeness C – might be built on the site; this is, however, now not to proceed.

In 1958 an eastbound train, headed by Class O1 No 31246, is pictured passing the signal box at Ore as a westbound train approaches Mount Pleasant Tunnel. Allocated to Ashford between November 1956 and June 1959, the 4-4-0 was finally withdrawn in early March 1961 from Nine Elms. On the extreme right of the photograph can be seen the EMU depot that was situated to the north of the station; this was closed in May 1986 following the electrification of the line from Tonbridge to Hastings with its work transferred to St Leonards. The depot has subsequently been demolished. *Fred Ivey/Online Transport Archive*

The Ashford to Ore line is now something of an anachronism in that it is the only diesel-operated passenger service in Kent. Part of the Southern franchise since privatisation, the service is now operated by Class 171 DMUs following their introduction in 203. These replaced the Class 206 DEMUs that had been introduced to the line in the early 1960s when steam traction was eliminated. The Class 171s are also used on the Southern's only other diesel-operated route – the Uckfield branch – and are all based at Selhurst for maintenance purposes. This can, however, cause major problems for the Ashford-Hastings service in the event of a failure. There have been proposals for the line's electrification, most recently in 2021 when Network Rail proposed two possible options – one using bimodal trains and the other conventional third-rail electrification – costing up to some £550 million.

On Sunday 22 August 1982 Class 205 No 1113 departs from Hastings with the 15.50 service to Ashford. Alongside is Class 33 No 33053, which was booked to depart from the station with a special excursion to Aylesbury at 17.30. *J. Gotts*

The fact that the line has survived to mark its 175th anniversary is – given the very real threats that existed to its future for more than a decade – perhaps in itself a cause for celebration. Its future looks secure but decisions about investment will determine the next generation of traction to operate over it.

BR Standard Class 5s on the Southern

When initially planned, it was anticipated that two batches of the BR Standard Class 5 4-6-0s would be allocated to the Southern. These were Nos 73080-89 of Lot 8241 to be constructed at Derby during 1955 and Nos 73110-119 of Lot 403 to be completed at Doncaster during the same year. The Derby-built batch were equipped with BR1B flush 4,725 gallon tenders (Nos 1282-91); as these locomotives were destined for the Southern – which possessed no water troughs – no water pick-up gear was installed. Nos 73110-119 were fitted with the larger capacity – 5,625 gallon – BR1F flush tender (Nos 1292-301), again without water pick-up gear. The locomotives were delivered in mixed traction livery of gloss black with cream, grey and red lining. The SR locomotives cost on average £21,750 each (for the Derby-built examples) and £21,183 for those completed at Doncaster. Although some of the class were subsequently repainted in green, none of those initially allocated to the Southern were so treated.

One of the class to emerge in lined green livery was No 73029, which is pictured here at Weymouth awaiting the departure of the LCGB 'Dorset Coast Express' to Waterloo. The 4-6-0 double-headed the train with Standard 2-6-0 No 76026 as far as Bournemouth Central where they were replaced by 'Merchant Navy' No 35003 *Royal Mail.* **New to Blackpool Central in January 1952, No 73029 had been a Western Region locomotive from October 1953 prior to being reallocated to Weymouth (Radipole) in October 1958 after the Southern had assumed responsibility for this ex-WR shed. Reallocated to Eastleigh (in September 1964) and Guildford (in June 1965), the locomotive was to end its operational life at Nine Elms following a transfer there in June 1966. No 73029 was one of the class that remained in service until the end of SR steam on 9 July 1967; indeed, it was noted in operation that day when it hauled an ECS working from Fratton to Clapham Junction.** *Alexander McBlain/Online Transport Archive*

The first of the class to reach the Southern were, however, three – Nos 73050-52 – that were allocated to Bath Green Park in June 1954 for service over the Somerset & Dorset route in place of Bulleid's Light Pacifics. Amongst services that they operated were the 'Pines Express'. During the summer of 1955 this trio was supplemented by four further examples – Nos 73047/49/73/74 – and, once the SR obtained its actual allocation, a number of these were also based on the S&D section. In order for the class to operate over the line, the allocated locomotives needed to be equipped with the Whitaker automatic tablet exchange equipment; this was fitted to the driver's side of the tender.

When new, Nos 73080-89 were all allocated to Stewarts Lane and employed primarily on Kent Coast services. The Doncaster-built batch were all based initially at Nine Elms, where they replaced 4-6-0s from the 'King Arthur' and 'Remembrance' classes; the majority of the redundant locomotives were soon withdrawn. Amongst services operated by the Nine Elms-based examples were the occasional turns on the 'Bournemouth Belle' when a Bulleid Pacific was unavailable.

A London Midland Region locomotive when new, No 73041 was reallocated to Stewarts Lane alongside No 73042 in exchange for two 'Britannias' – Nos 7004 *William Shakespeare* and 70014 *Iron Duke* – that were required by the LMR to support the accelerated timetable operated on the St Pancras to Manchester Central service. Although undated, this view of No 73041 entering Lewisham with a Down service must date to the brief period between June 1958, when it was transferred to Stewarts Lane, and June the following year when it migrated to the South Western and Nine Elms following the first phase of the Kent Coast electrification scheme. Transferred from Nine Elms to Weymouth (Radipole), No 73041 was then based for periods at both Eastleigh (twice) and Weymouth again, before a – brief – move in June 1965 saw it move to Guildford from where it was withdrawn later the same month. *Fred Ivey/Online Transport Archive*

The third of the class allocated from new to Bath Green Park was No 73051. On 10 March 1961 it is seen double-heading the southbound 'Pines Express' out of Bath up Devonshire Bank with 4-4-0 No 40569 acting as pilot locomotive. New from Derby in May 1954, No 73051 was to spend its BR operational career allocated to Green Park, but was not to last until the final closure of the Somerset & Dorset in March 1966, being withdrawn in August the previous year. *Alexander McBlain/Online Transport Archive*

Opposite top: Recorded on 4 April 1967, still looking in reasonable external condition despite the imminence of withdrawal, is No 73043 in Southampton Central station. Delivered to Patricroft in October 1953, the locomotive had been transferred to Sheffield Grimesthorpe shed in May 1958 and thence to Canklow in April the following year. One of a batch transferred to the Southern in December 1962, No 73043 was based at Eastleigh (December 1962 to December 1963 and from September 1964 until June 1965), Feltham (from December 1963 until September 1964) and Guildford from June 1965 until a final reallocation saw it move to Nine Elms in June 1966, from where it was withdrawn on 9 July 1967.

Bottom: Three of the class – Nos 73050-52 – were allocated to Bath Green Park from new in the spring of 1954 from Derby Works. Two of this trio – Nos 73050 and 73052 – are pictured here shortly after delivery, double-heading a southbound service over the River Avon at Bath with their home shed visible on the west side of the river. The former was to remain based at Green Park until April 1964 – except for a brief three-month stay at Gloucester Barnwood from August 1962 – when it was transferred to Llanelly for a brief period prior to a move to Shrewsbury later the same month. From there it moved to Agecroft in April 1966 for a six-month stay before a final reallocation saw it transferred to Patricroft in October 1966 from where it was withdrawn in June 1968. Purchased for preservation, the locomotive ran under its own steam from Manchester to Peterborough on 30 September 1968. The locomotive, now named *City of Peterborough*, has been based on the Nene Valley Railway for more than five decades. No 73052 was, however, to remain a Green Park-allocated locomotive for its entire BR career; stored in November 1964, the locomotive was formally withdrawn the following month. *Fred Ivey/Online Transport Archive*

Based for the early part of its BR career in and around Sheffield – at Millhouses and Canklow sheds – No 73065 was one of the class transferred to the Southern in December 1962. Based initially at Eastleigh, it was reallocated to Feltham in December the following year. Transferred to Nine Elms in November 1964, it was then based at Guildford for some 12 months – from June 1966 until June 1967 – when it returned to Nine Elms, from where it was withdrawn on 9 July 1967. Following the closure of Stewarts Lane to steam, Nine Elms provided the South Central with any required steam power and so it was, on 13 November 1966, that No 73065 was employed on the outward Southern Counties Touring Society 'West Country' special from Victoria to Westbury; the train is pictured here at Norwood Junction, where it was scheduled to pick up water between 10.32 and 10.46am.
Alexander McBlain/Online Transport Archive

Opposite top: **On 18 September 1961 No 73080 *Merlin* heads west at Deepcut with the 3.30pm service from Waterloo to Bournemouth West. By this date allocated to the ex-GWR Radipole shed at Weymouth – the locomotive's second period at that shed – No 73080 had initially been allocated to Norwood Junction when new in June 1955. It was also based at Nine Elms – from June to November 1959 – and Eastleigh for two months during the spring of 1961.** *Alexander McBlain/Online Transport Archive*

Bottom: **Recorded on the last day in June 1959 of main-line steam workings into Kent, No 73081 (named *Excalibur* in February 1961) makes a fine sight as it passes through Bromley South with a Down service. Allocated to Stewarts Lane when new from Derby Works in June 1955, No 73081 was one of the class to be transferred to the South Western as a result of the Kent Coast electrification scheme. Reallocated to Nine Elms in June 1959, the locomotive was finally withdrawn from Guildford, where it had been allocated since June 1965, at the end of July 1966.**
Peter N. Williams/Online Transport Archive

On 18 March 1956, when less than a year old, Stewarts Lane-based No 73084 (named *Tintagel* in November 1959) is pictured at Bickley Junction with the 12.35pm service from Victoria to Ramsgate. Reallocated to Nine Elms in June 1959, the locomotive spent a month at Feltham before a final transfer in November 1965 saw it migrate further west – to Eastleigh – from where it was withdrawn only a month later.
Peter N. Williams/Online Transport Archive

Opposite top: **Recorded during 1959 (but before August when it was named *Camelot*), No 73082 is seen at Eltham Park with a Down service; this station closed on 17 March 1985 when it and Eltham Well Hall were replaced by the new Eltham station. New to Stewarts Lane, the locomotive was transferred to Nine Elms in June 1959 and to Guildford, where it remained until withdrawal, in June 1965. Taken out of service in June 1966, No 73082 was sold for scrap to Woodham Bros. Languishing in the Barry scrapyard until January 1979, when it was rescued by the 73082 Camelot Locomotive Society (which had been established in March 1974 to try and secure it for preservation), the locomotive was moved to the Bluebell Railway in October 1979. Restoration took 16 years, but No 73082 re-entered service in October 1995. At the time of writing it forms part of the Bluebell's operational fleet.**
Fred Ivey/Online Transport Archive

Bottom: **No 73083, named *Pendragon* in October 1959, is seen here with an Up relief boat train at Kemsing in May that year. Allocated to Stewarts Lane from new until the first phase of the Kent Coast electrification in June 1959, the locomotive was then based at Nine Elms until September 1964 and then, after two months at Feltham, a final transfer saw it reallocated to Weymouth from where it was withdrawn in early September 1966.** *Derek Cross*

Recorded at the head of the 9.48am service to Bournemouth on 17 March 1966 at Surbiton is No 73085 *Melisande***. Allocated to Nine Elms from June 1959 until October 1965 and again from June 1966 until withdrawal at the start of July 1967, No 73085 was new to Stewarts Lane. During its time on the South Western, the locomotive was also briefly based at Feltham for a month in late 1965 and for seven months at Eastleigh from late 1965 until June 1966.**
Neil Davenport/Online Transport Archive

Opposite top: **In early 1958 No 73086 (named** *The Green Knight* **in December 1959) awaits departure from Bromley South. Allocated to only two sheds during its operational life – Stewarts Lane from new and Nine Elms from June 1959 – No 73086 was withdrawn in early October 1966.**
Peter N. Williams/Online Transport Archive

Bottom: **Looking in excellent external condition, No 73087** *Linette* **is seen at Clapham Junction on 25 March 1963 with empty coaching stock from Waterloo station. One of the more well-travelled of the class, No 73087 was delivered new to Stewarts Lane, where it remained for about a year. In August 1956 it was reallocated to Bath Green Park. Over the next five years it was reallocated to Eastleigh, back to Stewarts Lane, Nine Elms (twice) and Green Park (four times). In the summer of 1961 it returned to Nine Elms for three years – its single longest stay at a single shed – before being transferred to Feltham for a month in September 1964 and then to Eastleigh. A final move, in June 1965, saw the locomotive reallocated to its sixth shed – Guildford – from where it was withdrawn in October 1966.** *Alexander McBlain/Online Transport Archive*

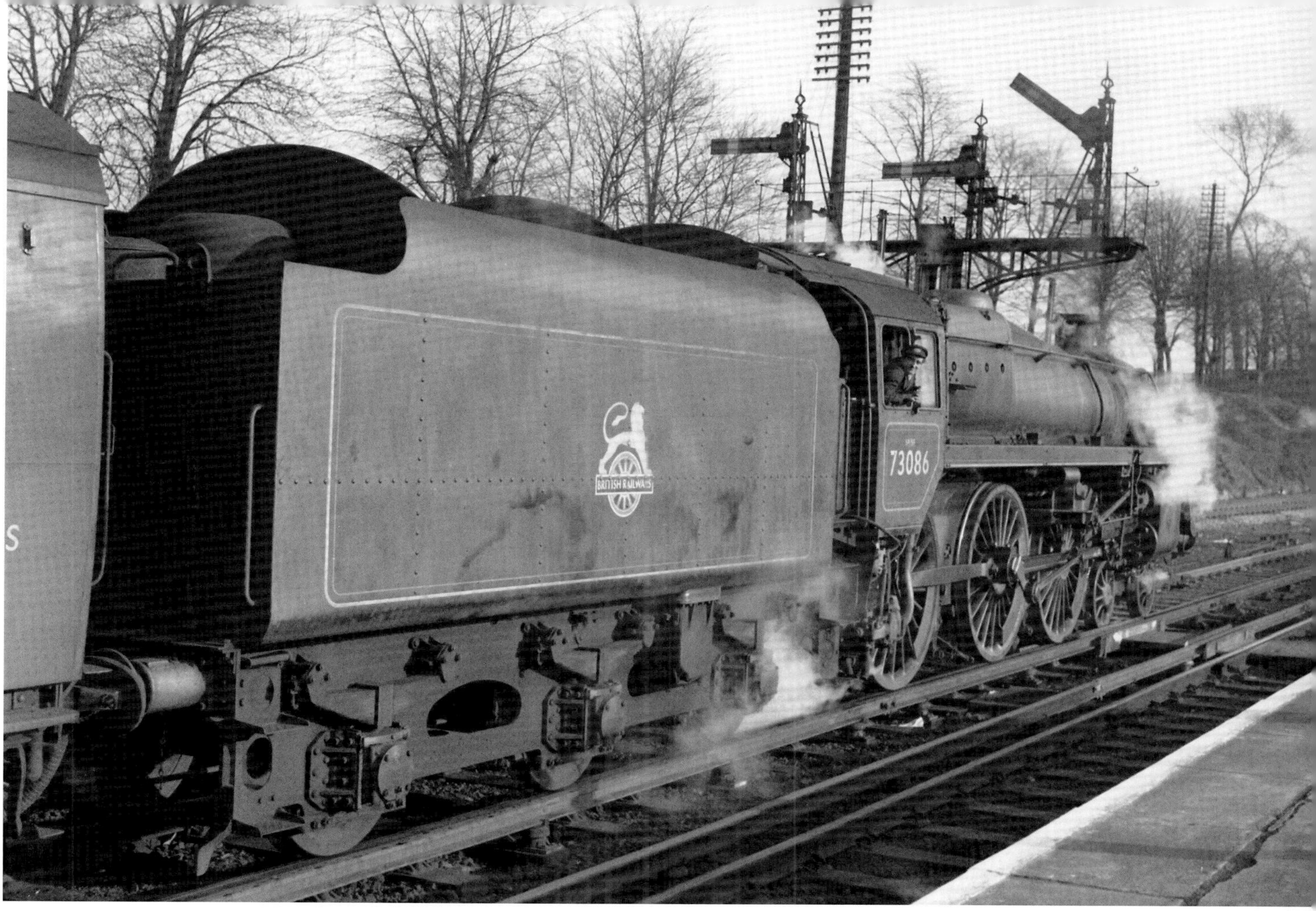
73086
BRITISH RAILWAYS

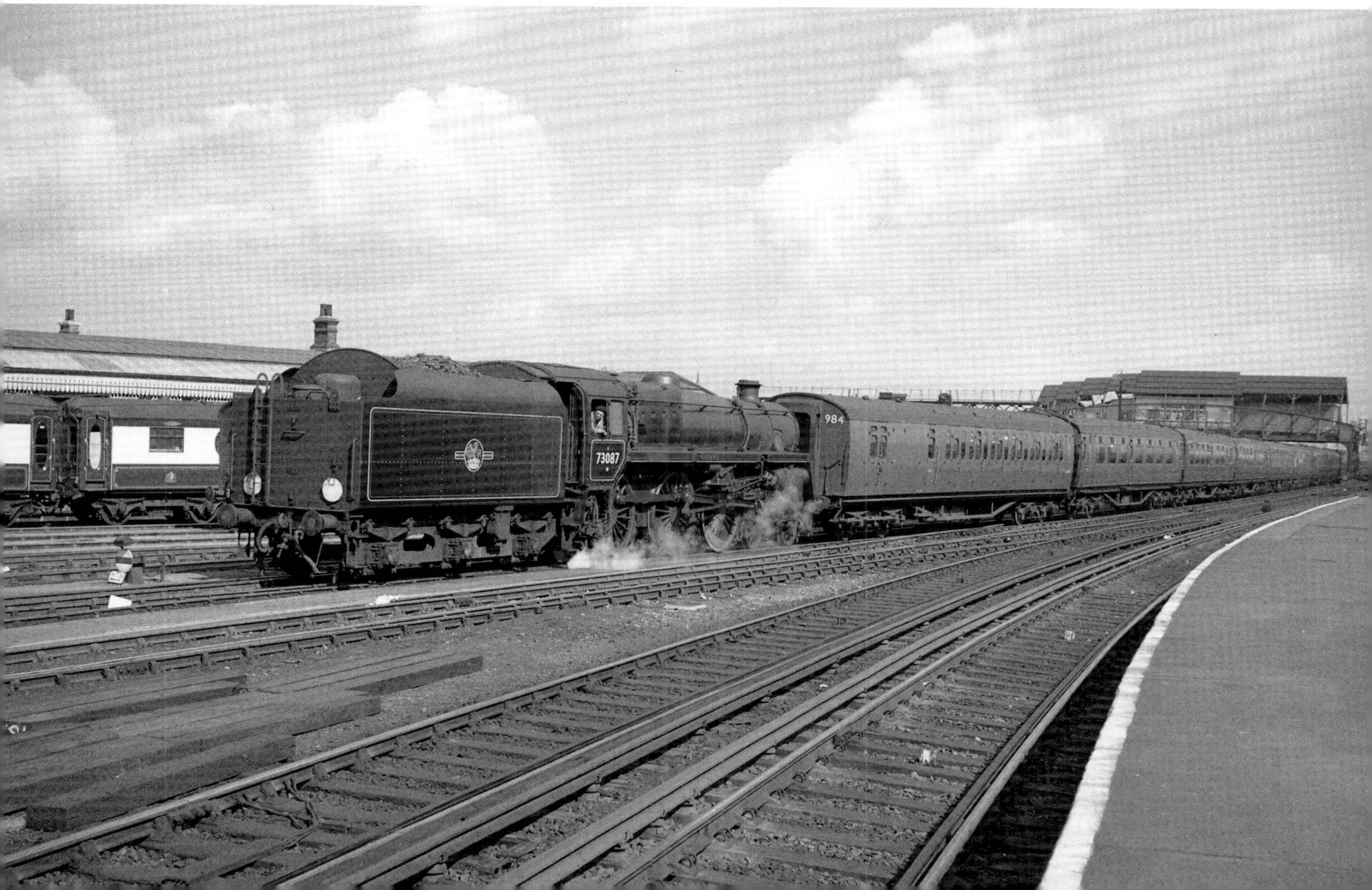
73087
984

In the early summer of 1957 the Southern had 25 of the class allocated: five (Nos 73047/49-52) at Bath Green Park, two (Nos 73087 and 73116) at Eastleigh, nine at Nine Elms (Nos 73110-115/117-119) and nine at Stewarts Lane (Nos 73080-86/88/89). With the redrawn regional boundaries in early 1958, the Southern lost control of Bath Green Park to the Western but acquired responsibility for Weymouth Radipole; in order to improve locomotive flexibility, five 'Hall' class 4-6-0s – which were not cleared to operate over the section from Basingstoke to Waterloo – were exchanged for an additional five Standard Class 5s – Nos 73017/18/20/22/29.

The next significant change occurred in the summer of 1959 with the completion of the first phase of the Kent Coast Electrification scheme. This displaced – either for withdrawal or transfer – a significant number of locomotives, including the Standard Class 5s, from the South Eastern, although the failure of a number of the new electric (future Class 71) locomotives in early 1960 saw a handful of the class return to the South Eastern briefly. Modernisation elsewhere – this time on the Eastern – saw further Standard 5s transferred to the Southern in late 1962; these were Nos 73002/16/43/46/65/74/155. Of these, two – Nos 73046 and 73074 – were initially based at

Nine Elms with the remainder going to Eastleigh. In the early autumn of the following year, Feltham gained its first allocation of the class – for use on freight traffic – when Nos 73167-171 were transferred from the North Eastern; these were supplemented by transfers from elsewhere in the region so that by January 1964 Feltham had an allocation of nine. The remaining 30 Southern-based Class 5s were allocated at this stage to Nine Elms (21: with the closure of Stewarts Lane to steam in September 1963, Nine Elms provided any steam that the South Central might require) and Weymouth (nine).

By January 1965, the Southern's allocation of the class had declined to 34; these were based at Eastleigh (19), Nine Elms (nine) and Weymouth (six). The spring of 1965 saw Guildford acquire its first allocation of the class and, in January 1966, four Southern sheds had an allocation of the class: Eastleigh (nine) Guildford (13), Nine Elms (one) and Weymouth (eight). By January 1967, withdrawals had reduced the Southern's allocation to 18; these were based at Eastleigh (two), Guildford (six), Nine Elms (six) and Weymouth (four). The last examples of the class were transferred from Eastleigh and Weymouth sheds to Guildford in April 1967. These were finally withdrawn with the end of Southern steam on 9 July 1967.

Pictured passing Southampton Junction signal box on 11 August 1964 and about to cross over the disused level crossing is No 73088 *Joyous Gard* with a Down train. New to Stewarts Lane at the start of September 1955, the locomotive was to spend five months – between May and October 1958 – based at Bath Green Park before being reallocated to Nine Elms; a final move – in October 1965 – saw the 4-6-0 move to Guildford from where it was withdrawn at the start of October 1966. The box closed in 1966 and was subsequently demolished. *Tim Stubbs/Online Transport Archive*

Number	New	Name and date named*	Withdrawn	Notes
73002	May 1951	N/A	March 1967	Transferred to the Southern December 1962
73003	May 1951	N/A	December 1965	Loaned to the Southern and based at Nine Elms May to July 1953; in green livery post-November 1959
73016	September 1951	N/A	December 1966	Transferred to the Southern December 1962
73017	September 1951	N/A	October 1964	Transferred to the Southern September 1958
73018	October 1951	N/A	July 1967	Transferred to the Southern September 1958; in green livery post-December 1958
73020	October 1951	N/A	July 1967	Transferred to the Southern September 1958
73022	October 1951	N/A	April 1967	Transferred to the Southern October 1958
73029	January 1952	N/A	July 1967	Transferred to the Southern October 1958; in green livery post-July 1963
73041	October 1953	N/A	June 1965	Transferred to the Southern June 1959
73042	October 1953	N/A	August 1965	Transferred to the Southern June 1958; involved in the collision at Eastbourne on 25 August 1958 with Class 6PUL No 3014
73043	October 1953	N/A	July 1967	Transferred to the Southern December 1962
73046	November 1953	N/A	June 1964	Transferred to the Southern December 1962
73047	December 1953	N/A	December 1964	Based at Bath Green Park August 1955 to July 1964
73049	December 1953	N/A	March 1965	Based at Bath Green Park August 1955 to April 1960 and from July 1962 until October 1964; in green livery from August 1963
73050	April 1954	N/A	June 1968	Based at Bath Green Park April 1954 until August 1962 and from November 1962 until April 1964; preserved
73051	May 1954	N/A	August 1965	Based at Bath Green Park for entire operational life; in green livery from September 1963
73052	May 1954	N/A	December 1964	Based at Bath Green Park for entire operational life
73065	October 1954	N/A	July 1967	Transferred to the Southern December 1962
73073	December 1954	N/A	November 1967	Based at Bath Green Park April 1955 to August 1955
73074	December 1954	N/A	September 1964	Based at Bath Green Park April 1955 to August 1955
73080	June 1955	*Merlin* February 1961*	December 1966	
73081	June 1955	*Excalibur* February 1961*	July 1966	
73082	June 1955	*Camelot* August 1959*	September 1966	Preserved
73083	July 1955	*Pendragon* October 1959*	September 1966	
73084	July 1955	*Tintagel* November 1959*	December 1965	
73085	August 1955	*Melisande* August 1959*	July 1967	
73086	August 1955	*The Green Knight* December 1959*	October 1966	
73087	August 1955	*Linette* June 1961*	October 1966	
73088	September 1955	*Joyous Gard* May 1961*	October 1966	
73089	September 1955	*Maid of Astolat* May 1959*	September 1966	
73110	September 1955	*The Red Knight* January 1960*	January 1967	
73111	October 1955	*King Uther* December 1960*	October 1965	
73112	October 1955	*Morgan Le Fay* April 1960*	June 1965	
73113	October 1955	*Lyonnesse* December 1959	January 1967	
73114	November 1955	*Etarre* April 1960*	June 1966	
73115	November 1955	*King Pellinore* February 1960*	March 1967	
73116	November 1955	*Iseult* October 1960* (officially September 1962)	November 1964	
73117	November 1955	*Vivien* April 1961*	March 1967	
73118	December 1955	*King Leodegrance* February 1960*	July 1967	
73119	December 1955	*Elaine* June 1959*	March 1967	
73155	December 1956	N/A	July 1967	Transferred to the Southern December 1962
73167	April 1957	N/A	August 1965	Based at Feltham September 1963 to September 1964
73168	April 1957	N/A	December 1965	Transferred to the Southern September 1963
73169	April 1957	N/A	October 1966	Transferred to the Southern September 1963
73170	May 1957	N/A	June 1966	Transferred to the Southern September 1963
73171	May 1957	N/A	October 1966	Transferred to the Southern September 1963

* The month in which the locomotive departed from Eastleigh Works to the running shed

No 73111 *King Uther* is recorded here departing from Bramley with the 1.48pm service from Reading General to Portsmouth on 6 March 1961. Allocated to Nine Elms from new in October 1955 until reallocation to Eastleigh in September 1964, No 73110 was withdrawn in October the following year – only the second of the named Class 5s to be taken out of service. *Alexander McBlain/Online Transport Archive*

Opposite top: With its 70D – Eastleigh – shedplate prominent, No 73089 *Maid of Astolat* was employed in shunting operations at Guildford on 26 February 1966; by this date, however, the locomotive was actually allocated to Guildford and had been since October the previous year. New to Stewarts Lane in September 1955, the locomotive had been reallocated to Nine Elms in June 1958 and to Eastleigh in September 1964. When recorded here, the 4-6-0 was approaching the end of its short operational life; it was withdrawn in late September 1966. *Neil Davenport/Online Transport Archive*

Bottom: On 13 September 1958 Nine Elms-allocated No 73110 (named *The Red Knight* in January 1960) is pictured at the head of the 11.54am local from Waterloo to Salisbury at Deepcut. Based in west London for almost a decade, the locomotive was initially reallocated to Eastleigh in September 1964; it remained there until October the following year when it was transferred to Guildford, its final shed. One of a handful of the Southern-based locomotives to survive into 1967, No 73110 was not to enjoy the New Year for long as it was withdrawn by the end of January.
Alexander McBlain/Online Transport Archive

An unnamed No 73112 – it acquired the name *Morgan Le Fay* in April 1960 – is pictured with a Waterloo to Bournemouth service at Farnborough. Apart from a brief one-month sojourn at Eastleigh during the autumn of 1965, No 73112 was to be based at Nine Elms for its entire operational career, from new in October 1955 through to withdrawal in late June 1965. *Derek Cross*

Opposite top: **Another view at Deepcut – this time on 1 September 1962 – sees No 73113 *Lyonnesse* heading westwards with the 9.24am service from Waterloo to Weymouth. Allocated to Nine Elms when new, the locomotive was reallocated to Eastleigh in September 1964; it was to remain there for about a year before a final move saw it transferred to Radipole shed in Weymouth. Another of the class to make it into 1967 – just – No 73113 succumbed by the end of January that year.** *Alexander McBlain/Online Transport Archive*

Bottom: **Pictured passing the disused Down platform at Bramshott Halt – a station that closed in May 1946 – with the 1.54pm service from Waterloo to Basingstoke is No 73114 *Etarre*. Another of the class to spend the bulk of its operational career from new at Nine Elms, No 73114 was allocated for a year to Eastleigh before a final reallocation, in October 1965, saw it move to Radipole, from where it was withdrawn in early June 1966.**
Alexander McBlain/Online Transport Archive

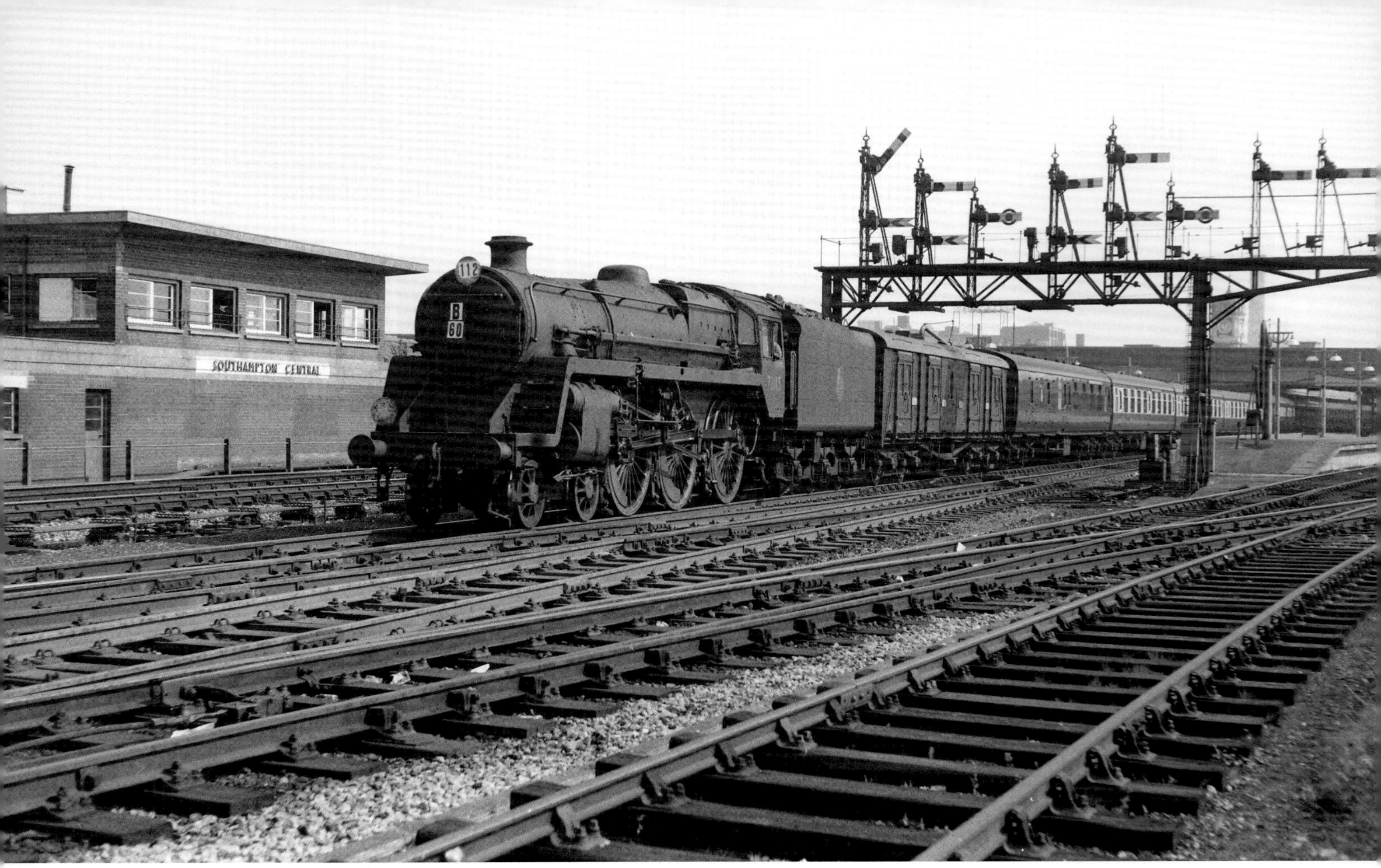
SOUTHAMPTON CENTRAL
112
B
60

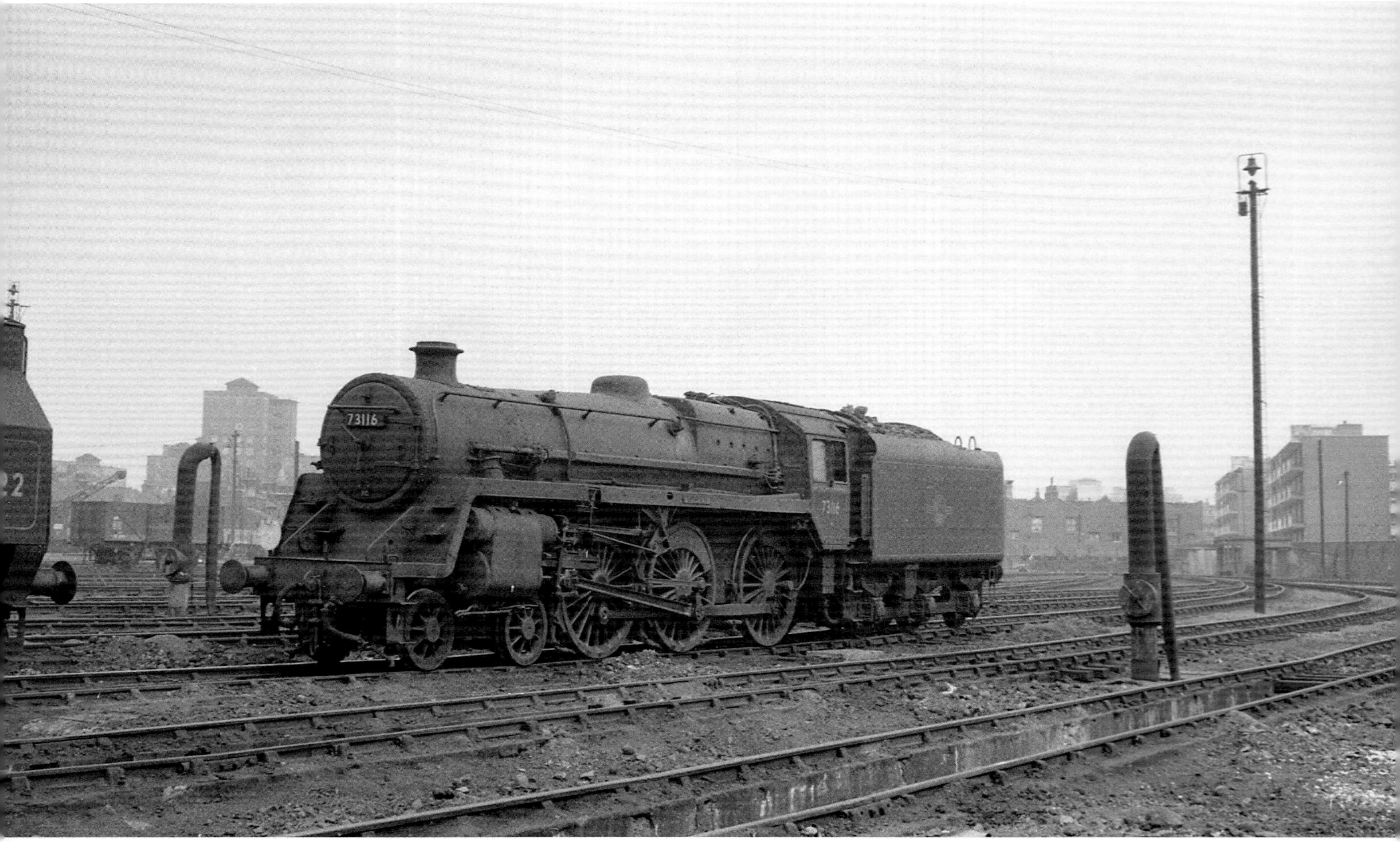
73116

On a damp day in early 1959 – 24 February to be exact – No 73117 (later to be named *Vivien*) awaits departure from Basingstoke with the 9.30am service from Waterloo to Weymouth. New to Nine Elms in November 1955, the locomotive was to remain allocated to that shed until September 1965 when it was transferred to Eastleigh. It returned to Nine Elms in June 1966 where it remained for four months until a final move, in October 1966, saw it reallocated to Guildford from where it was withdrawn in mid-March 1967. *Alexander McBlain/Online Transport Archive*

Opposite top: In June 1960, No 73115, which was allocated to Nine Elms at the time, is seen passing the box at Southampton Central with a boat train to the old docks. The locomotive was reallocated to Eastleigh in September 1964. Following a return to Nine Elms in June 1966, a final transfer, in October that year, saw it move to Guildford, from where it was withdrawn in March 1967. *Derek Cross*

Bottom: Pictured on shed at Nine Elms alongside BR Standard 2-6-2T No 82022 is No 73116 *Iseult*. New to Nine Elms in mid-November 1955, the locomotive was reallocated to Bath Green Park in August 1956; except for the period of time between October 1956 and July 1957, when it was based at Eastleigh, and from October 1957 until June 1958, when it was again allocated to Nine Elms, No 73116 was to spend much of the next five years working over the Somerset & Dorset route. It returned to Nine Elms in April 1960, where it was to remain until September 1964 when a final move saw it reallocated to Eastleigh from where it was withdrawn two months later. *Phil Tatt/Online Transport Archive*

Seen on shed at Feltham on 27 April 1963 is No 73118 *King Leodegrance*. One of the class to survive until the end of Southern steam, No 73118 was delivered new to Nine Elms in December 1956; reallocated to Eastleigh in September 1964, it then passed to Nine Elms again in June 1966 before a final move – in October 1966 – saw it reallocated to Guildford. *Neil Davenport/Online Transport Archive*

Opposite top: **On 13 October 1957, No 73119 *Elaine* is pictured heading a Down service through New Malden station; this was only a month after the station had been officially renamed from simply Malden, the name it had carried for only two years, having been known as Malden for Coombe since November 1912. No 73119 had been, when recorded here, a Nine Elms-based locomotive since delivery in December 1955; it was to remain there until September 1964 when its only reallocation saw it move to Eastleigh, from where it was withdrawn in March 1967.**
Peter N. Williams/Online Transport Archive

Bottom: **In September 1963 five of the class were transferred from the North Eastern Region, where they had been allocated to sheds around Leeds. Numerically the first of this quintet was No 73167 which is pictured here outside Feltham shed alongside No D6549 towards the end of its relatively short life on the Southern. The five arrivals represented the first allocation of the Standard Class 5s to Feltham and were intended for use on freight traffic. No 73167 had been based at Holbeck prior to its reallocation; it was transferred to Shrewsbury in August 1964 from where it was withdrawn in early August 1965.** *Neil Davenport/Online Transport Archive*

Although it was not until the spring of 1965 that Guildford received its first allocation of the class, examples were regular visitors prior to that date. On 11 December 1964 No 73171 bearing its redundant 70B (Feltham) shedplate was present; the locomotive had been reallocated to Eastleigh the previous month. The 4-6-0 had been delivered new to York in May 1957 and had been based at Holbeck and then Royston before its transfer southwards in September 1963. The locomotive was withdrawn from Eastleigh in early October 1966. *Neil Davenport/Online Transport Archive*

Opposite top: **On 30 April 1964 No 73169 is pictured at Fleet with an Up train of track material. New in April 1957, the Standard had been based at no fewer than five North Eastern Region sheds – York (North), Scarborough, Holbeck, Neville Hill and Wakefield – before its transfer to Feltham in September 1963. It was to remain based there until a final reallocation, in November 1964, saw it migrate westwards to Eastleigh, from where it was withdrawn in early October 1966.** *Neil Davenport/Online Transport Archive*

Bottom: **Pictured at Portsmouth & Southsea with the 9.30am service to Cardiff is No 73170. Transferred from Royston to Feltham in September 1963, the locomotive had, by the date of this photograph, been reallocated to Eastleigh (in November 1964) where it remained until withdrawal in mid-June 1966.** *Tim Stubbs/Online Transport Archive*

Tribute to the Class 455s

In 1980, the Southern Region obtained authorisation to acquire replacement rolling stock for its suburban services; these were scheduled to permit the transfer of the Class 508 units to Merseyside – see *Southern Way 72* – and to replace older slam-door stock (Classes 405 and 415). Based around the Mark 3 carriage, the new stock was originally to be designated Class 510 as a DC version of the Class 317 AC units but this was subsequently revised to Class 455. The AC stock had been fitted with the chopper control system but this was deemed unsuitable for third-rail operation and, as a result, the DC stock was equipped with the GEC Traction camshaft-control system.

Work on the construction of the units was placed with the Holgate Road, York, Works of BREL, with construction commencing in late 1981. The first sets to be completed were initially sent to Wolverton Works from October 1982 in order to fit a wheel-slip over-ride protection system. Three batches were completed between 1982 and 1985; the first of these – Class 455/8 – comprised 46 units for the South Central and 28 for the South Western and were built between 1982 and 1984. The second batch – the Class 455/7 – was delivered during 1984 and 1985 for the South Western; these were completed as three-car sets but were increased to four-car units by the inclusion of redundant TSOs from the Class 508 stock prior to the latter's transfer northwards. The final 20 – the Class 455/9s – were delivered in 1985 again to the South Western.

When the class was first introduced, the '455s' appeared in blue and grey as evinced by No 5728, seen departing from Wimbledon on 29 September 1988 with the 10.12 service from Waterloo to Guildford. The different roof line shown by the ex-Class 508 TSO, in this case No 71527 (ex-No 508002), is all too evident.
Bernard Harrison/Charles Firminger Collection/Online Transport Archive

The interior of DMSO No 77597 from set No 5810 on 22 August 1983 at Waterloo station. The majority of the seating for the class was arranged as 3+2, resulting in a seating capacity of 316 standard class passengers. *Geoffrey Tribe/Online Transport Archive*

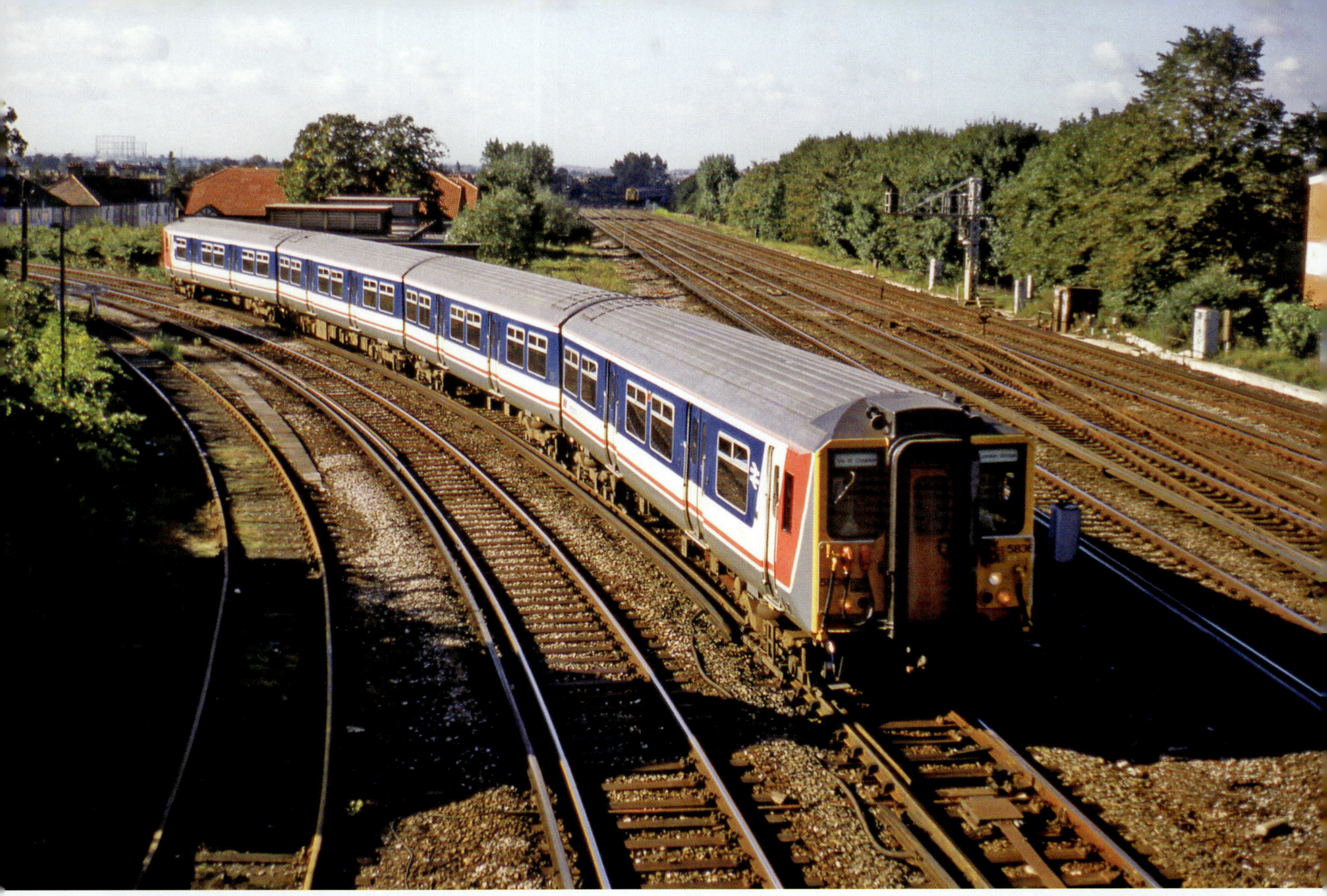

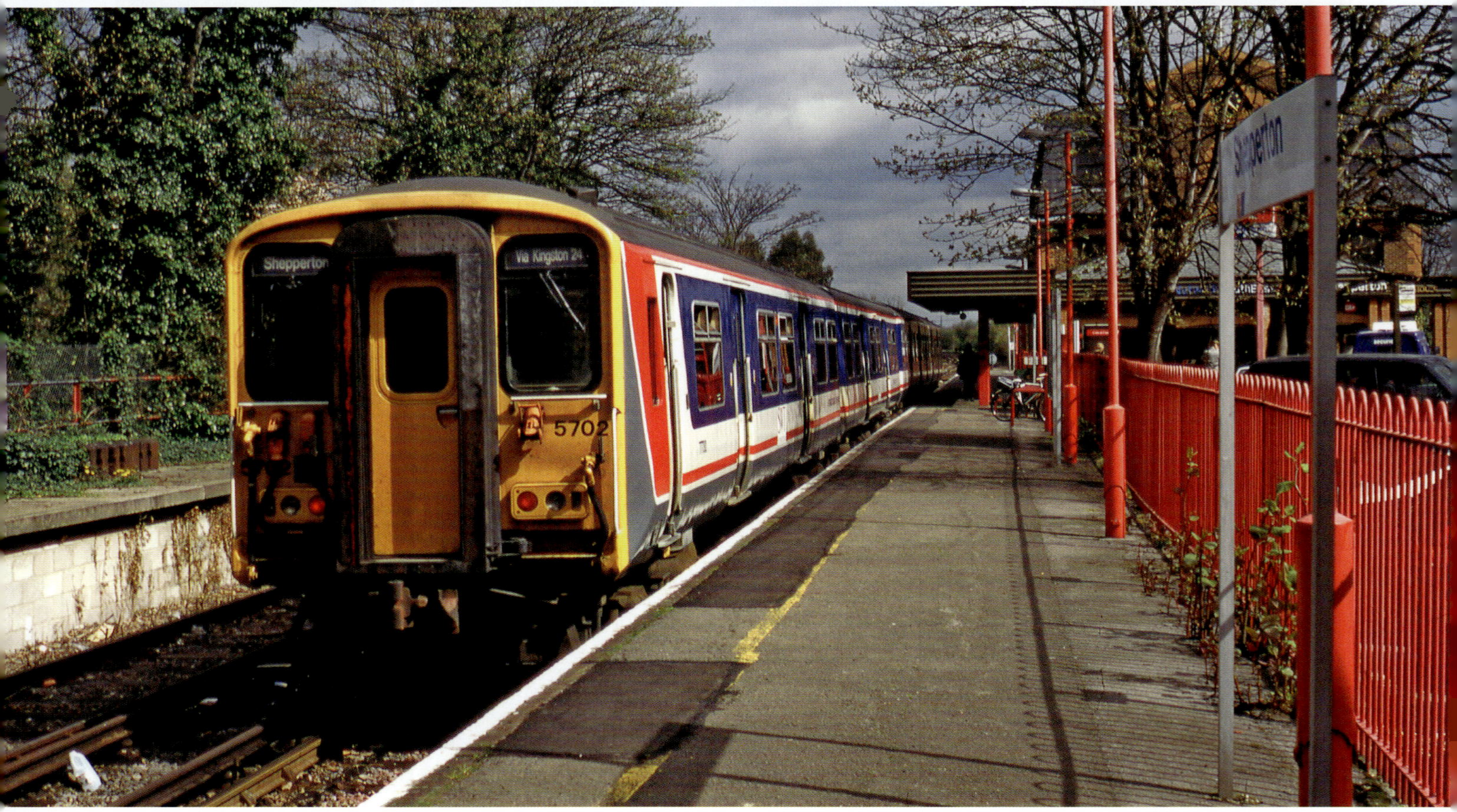
Shepperton
Via Kingston 24
5702
Shepperton

Pictured in the first iteration of the South West Trains livery at Waterloo on 19 February 200 is No 5723. The franchisee started to adopt the modified former Network SouthEast livery on the class from September 1996 onwards. *Geoffrey Tribe/Online Transport Archive*

As constructed, the Class 455s had similar bodyshells to the Classes 317 and 318 that were constructed in steel; this differed from the aluminium alloy used in those units – such as the Class 508s – that had been based on the prototype 'PEP' stock. As was traditional with the Southern's EMU replacement policy, the class incorporated equipment recovered from older – and withdrawn – rolling stock. This included traction equipment recovered from redundant Class 4SUBs. A total of 505 carriages were constructed; these, combined with the 43 TSOs reused from the Class 508 stock, resulted in a total of 137 four-car sets. As the units were designed primarily for inner suburban services, they lacked first class accommodation, air conditioning and lavatories. When new, the power cars were equipped with four English Electric 507-20J motors, each rated at 153kW (205hp). The units were limited to a maximum speed of 75mph.

Opposite top: **The creation of Network SouthEast saw the introduction of a new white, blue and red livery and the entire fleet was eventually to carry this scheme, as evinced by No 5836 approaching Wimbledon on 29 September 1988 with the 09.49 service from West Croydon. Passenger trains over the line to West Croydon were withdrawn on 2 June 1997 prior to conversion of the route to form part of the Croydon Tramlink network.** *Bernard Harrison/Charles Firminger Collection/Online Transport Archive*

Bottom: **On 3 April 1997 No 5702 stands in the platform at Shepperton awaiting departure with the 12.27 service to Waterloo. Although post-privatisation, the unit retains its Network SouthEast livery. Class 455 units were introduced to the branch on 28 March 1983 some five years before the completion of the new station building visible in this view. Clock House, as the office block that incorporated the new station, was for some years the home of Ian Allan Publishing.** *Bernard Harrison/Charles Firminger Collection/Online Transport Archive*

During the first decade of the 21st century a number of units appeared in non-standard promotional liveries for a variety of businesses and events. South West Trains No 5853 carried a livery promoting Côtes du Rhone wines for a period; it is pictured here on the 10.39 service from Hampton Court to Waterloo at Raynes Park on 15 March 2003. *Alex Dasi-Sutton*

The first units were delivered to Strawberry Hill depot in 1982. The first to be brought south was No 5805; this was collected by Class 73 No 73102 – which had travelled light engine northwards – on 10 November 1982 and was officially unveiled at Waterloo station six days later. The new unit, although fitted with third-rail pick-up shoes, was loco-hauled to and from the station and was not permitted to operate under its own power. After its display at Waterloo, the unit returned to Strawberry Hill and then to Wolverton for final completion work. Delivery in numbers to Strawberry Hill commenced on 20 December 1982 and work commenced on their commissioning.

Initially all units – both for the South Central and the South Western – were allocated to Wimbledon depot; the Class 455/8s destined for the former were reallocated to Selhurst in 1986 following modification work to the depot. Passenger services commenced on 28 March 1983. The type was employed on suburban services, such as the South Western's routes to Windsor & Eton Riverside, Weybridge, Shepperton and Hampton Court and could operate either as four-car sets or two units together. Each unit, as new, could accommodate 316 standard class passengers with seating normally 3+2.

When delivered, the units were completed in BR blue and grey livery; with the launch of Network SouthEast in 1986, the stock was to appear gradually in the grey, red, white and blue livery that was adopted for NSE.

Towards the end of their BR career, a number of the Class 455/9s underwent modification as testbeds. Two units were modified in 1990 with chopper control supplied by Brush and GEC to test its suitability; the work showed marginal performance enhancement with the latter but reliability problems with the former. As a result the equipment was removed and the units reverted to their original equipment. Four years later, two TSOs were fitted with plug doors in connection with planning for the original – failed – Crossrail project. However, it was found that the modification weakened the structure with the result that one reverted to its original doors whilst the other (No 71725) was withdrawn and replaced by a modified TSO from Class 210 DEMU No 60400 (renumbered 67400). The original carriage was used as a source of spare parts at Eastleigh; prior to being scrapped in 2005 it was used to demonstrate the new overall red livery adopted by South West Trains for its inner suburban services.

With privatisation looming following the Royal Assent given to the Railway Act on 5 November 1993, the ownership of the Class 455s was split between Eversholt (that received the 46 Class 455/8s used by South Central) and Porterbrook (all those units destined for the South Western franchise).

On 13 October 1996 the South Central franchise was taken over by Connex SouthCentral; the new operator's rolling stock including 46 Class 455 units. Of these, 16 were eventually repainted in the franchisee's yellow and white livery. Here No 5802 is seen at Dorking North on 31 August 2003. *Geoffrey Tribe/Online Transport Archive*

In 2002 the country celebrated the Golden Jubilee of HM Queen Elizabeth II; to mark this anniversary, SWT applied a special livery to No 5868 featuring Hampton Court Palace. It is seen here on 14 August 2004 with, appropriately, the 09.39 service from Hampton Court to Waterloo at Raynes Park. Some years later No 5868 would reappear in a version of its original BR blue and grey livery; see page 53. *Alex Dasi-Sutton*

The last day of Class 455 operation on Southern was on Saturday, 14 May 2022. Whilst a significant number of units were operational on this final day, two – Nos 455841 and 455835 – were employed on a farewell tour: the 'Metro Marauder'. The train is pictured here at Crawley. Co-organised by Southern and the Branch Line Society, the special travelled widely over the Southern network, including a number of locations not normally served by the type. It departed from Victoria at 09.02 and arrived back there at 19.09 some 20 minutes late. The two units employed were despatched to Newport the following week. *Alex Dasi-Sutton*

The first franchise to commence operation was South West Trains – a subsidiary of the Stagecoach Group – which was launched on 4 February 1996. Initially the new operators modified the NSE livery but replaced the grey with white and incorporated red and orange bands. Between November 2004 and March 2008, the SWT fleet underwent refurbishment at the Bombardier works at Ashford; the work included replacement of the seats and repainting in the new red livery. A further modification – commencing in June 2014 – saw the original DC motors replaced by more powerful AC units supplied by Vossloh Kiepe. The work also involved new control equipment and regenerative braking courtesy of brake controllers manufactured by Knorr-Bremse.

All of the franchise's Class 455s passed to South Western Railway with the change of franchisee in August 2017. However, the new owners intended to acquire new stock to replace the ageing units that they inherited. Orders were placed with Bombardier for 90 Class 701 Arterio units: 60 10-car (Class 701/0) and 30 five-car (Class 701/5). These were manufactured at Litchurch Lane, Derby. However, problems caused by Covid and other factors resulted in considerable delays to the type's introduction and it was not until 30 September 2024 that public service commenced. The issues with the Class 701 programme undoubtedly meant a prolonged life for the '455s'. However, all good things – even Class 455s – come to an end and as the new stock was progressively accepted into service, so the Class 455s were gradually withdrawn. Initially it had been hoped that all would have been taken out of service by the end of 2025 and, in expectation of this, a farewell tour was operated on 21 December 2025. However, SWR retained a number of units into the new year and it was not until 20 March 2026 that the class operated its final revenue earning services.

Opposite top: **Also seen at Raynes Park, but on 14 April 2007 with the 11 08 service from Guildford to Waterloo, is No 5869. This was one of two units – the other being No 5905 – that were used to promote the Royal British Legion poppy appeal.** *Alex Dasi-Sutton*

Bottom: **One of the most popular tourist attractions served by South West Trains was Legoland at Windsor, which opened on 17 March 1996, and it was perhaps inevitable that a unit would emerge promoting it. Bearing Legoland livery is No 5856, which is recorded here at Clapham Junction with the 11.24 service from Waterloo to Dorking on 22 September 2006.** *Alex Dasi-Sutton*

Following their wholesale withdrawal in May 2022, Southern's units made their way towards the scrapyard. Pictured on 22 June 2022 heading towards Stewarts Lane from Hove on the Redhill avoiding line with the 11.43 5Z55 ECS are three units: Nos 455801, 455823 and (at the rear) No 455844. The photographer comments: 'From memory despite being a funeral train these were shifting. Sad because Southern sort of rid themselves of 455s and 313s plus reduced the coaches in 171s at roughly the same time. Very little to replace them. Services were trimmed back.' *Alex Dasi-Sutton*

Whilst the majority of the class passed to South West Trains, Connex South Central acquired 46. The new franchisee – initially Connex when it took over on 26 May 1996 but renamed Connex South Central from 13 October 1996 – repainted 16 of the units into its white and yellow livery before it was stripped of the franchise on 25 August 2001. The new franchisee South Central – a subsidiary of Govia – was rebranded as Southern in May 203 and a handful of units appeared in the franchise's white and green livery. All 46 units were refurbished at Eastleigh Works by Alstom over a two-year period commencing in February 2004. The work included replacing the seats and the installation of air conditioning in the driver's cabs (achieved through the removal of the cab end gangways). Between August 2012 and December 2013, the units underwent a further refurbishment, emerging in Southern's two-tone green and white livery. A final upgrade – starting in January 2018 – was designed to make them compatible with the requirements of the Disability Discrimination Act 205.

The Southern's Class 455s were taken out of service in May 2022, following a farewell tour that ran on 4 May that year. They were not directly replaced – in the post-Covid world there was a reduced requirement for stock when passenger services started to be restored post-lockdowns – but their duties were taken over by Class 377 stock.

With withdrawal came the inexorable procession of the stock to store and to the scrapyard; fortunately, one unit – No 5871 – has been secured for preservation by the Southern Electric Traction Group. The unit moved to Strawberry Hill on 14 January 2026 where it underwent a full mechanical inspection and a thorough 'D' examination. The group, which also looks after Class 4VEP No 3417, intends to maintain the '455' in operational condition.

Number	DMSO	MSO	TSO	DTSO	Notes
5701	77727	63783	71545	77728	
5702	77729	62784	71547	77730	
5703	77731	62785	71540	77732	
5704	77733	62786	71548	77734	
5705	77735	62787	71565	77736	
5706	77737	62788	71534	77738	
5707	77739	62789	71536	77740	
5708	77741	62790	71560	77742	
5709	77743	62791	71532	77744	
5710	77745	62792	71566	77746	
5711	77747	62793	71542	77748	
5712	77749	62794	71546	77750	
5713	77751	62795	71567	77752	
5714	77753	62796	71539	77754	
5715	77755	62797	71535	77756	
5716	77757	62798	71564	77758	
5717	77759	62799	71528	77760	
5718	77761	62800	71557	77762	
5719	77763	62801	71558	77764	
5720	77765	62802	71568	77766	
5721	77767	62803	71553	77768	
5722	77769	62804	71533	77770	
5723	77771	62805	71526	77772	
5724	77773	62806	71561	77724	
5725	77775	62807	71541	77776	
5726	77777	62808	71556	77778	Suffered two significant failures of the upgraded electrical equipment
5727	77779	62809	71562	77780	
5728	77781	62810	71527	77782	
5729	77783	62811	71550	77784	
5730	77785	62812	71551	77866	Involved in a level crossing accident with a bus at Pooley Green on 17 October 2000
5731	77787	62813	71555	77788	
5732	77789	62814	71552	77790	
5733	77791	62815	71549	77792	
5734	77793	62816	71531	77794	
5735	77795	62817	71563	77796	
5736	77797	62818	71554	77798	
5737	77799	62819	71544	77800	
5738	77801	62820	71529	77802	
5739	77803	62821	71537	77804	
5740	77805	62822	71530	77806	
5741	77807	62823	71559	77808	
5742	77809	62824	71543	77810	
5743	77811	62825	71538	77812	Renumbered 5750 in May 1991 and named *Wimbledon Traincare Depot* when the achieved BS5750 quality services accreditation.

Number	DTSO	MSO	TSO	DTSO	
5801	77579	62709	71637	77580	Latterly operated with DTSO 77627 in place of 77579 and TSO 71657
5802	77581	62710	71638	77582	Latterly operated with TSO 71664; collided with No 5820 at Gypsy Hill on 18 February 1090
5803	77583	62711	71639	77584	
5804	77585	62712	71640	77586	
5805	77587	62713	71641	77588	
5806	77589	62714	71642	77590	
5807	77591	62715	71643	77592	
5808	77593	62716	71644	77594	Latterly operated with DTSO 77637 in place of 77593
5809	77595	62717	71645	77596	Latterly operated with DTSOs 77623 and 77602 in place of 77595 and 77596 and TSO 71648
5810	77597	62718	71646	77598	
5811	77599	62719	71647	77600	
5812	77601	62720	71648	77602	Latterly operated with DTSOs 77595 and 77626 in place of 77601 and 77602 and TSO 71645
5813	77603	62721	71649	77604	
5814	77605	62722	71650	77606	
5815	77607	62723	71651	77608	
5816	77609	62724	71652	77610	Latterly operated with DTSO 77633 in place of 77610
5817	77611	62725	71653	77612	
5818	77613	62726	71654	77614	Latterly operated with DTSO 77632 in place of 77614
5819	77615	62727	71655	77616	
5820	77617	62728	71656	77618	Damaged on 18 February 1990 when it hit a tree at Gipsy Hill and derailed; it was then hit by No 5802
5821	77619	62729	71657	77620	
5822	77621	62730	71658	77622	
5823	77623	62731	71659	77624	Latterly operated with DTSOs 77601 and 77596 in place of 77623 and 77624
5824	77625	62732	71660	77626	Latterly operated with DTSOs 77593 and 77624 in place of 77625 and 77626
5825	77627	62733	71661	77628	Latterly operated with DTSO 77579 in place of 77627
5826	77629	62734	71662	77630	
5827	77631	62735	71663	77632	Latterly operated with DTSO 77610 and 77614 in place of 77631 and 77632
5828	77633	62736	71664	77634	Latterly operated with DTSO 77631 in place of 77633
5929	77635	62737	71665	77636	
5830	77637	62738	71666	77638	Latterly operated with DTSO 77625 in place of 77637
5831	77639	62739	71667	77640	
5832	77641	62740	71668	77642	
5833	77643	62741	71669	77644	
5834	77645	62742	71670	77646	
5835	77647	62743	71671	77648	Used on the farewell 'Metro Marauder' railtour
5836	77649	62744	71672	77650	
5837	77651	62745	71673	77652	
5838	77653	62746	71674	77654	
5839	77655	62747	71675	77656	
5840	77657	62748	71676	77658	
5841	77659	62749	71677	77660	Used on the farewell 'Metro Marauder' railtour
5842	77661	62750	71678	77662	
5843	77663	62751	71679	77664	
5844	77665	62752	71680	77666	
5845	77667	62753	71681	77668	
5846	77669	62754	71682	77670	

In 2024 No 5868 was repainted into a version of its original BR blue and grey livery; it was not wholly authentic, however, as modern regulations required that the doors be painted all-over grey. The unit is seen here in the company of No 5719 forming the 10.47 service from Waterloo to Chessington South on 6 March 2025 at Wimbledon. Later in the year the celebrity unit was to make the long journey north for display at Derby Litchurch Lane as part of the 'Greatest Gathering' event held there as part of Rail 200. At the time of writing, the unit was still in store at Derby with preservation being a possibility. *Alex Dasi-Sutton*

On 17 September 2025 No 37884 is pictured at Clapham Junction with the 10.35 (5Q86) service from Wimbledon Park to the Simms scrapyard – since closed – at Newport Docks with two units – Nos 5913 and 5911 – on their final journey. *Alex Dasi-Sutton*

Number	DMSO	MSO	TSO	DTSO	
5847	77671	62755	71683	77672	
5847	77671	62755	71683	77672	
5848	77673	62756	71684	77674	
5849	77675	62757	71685	77676	
5850	77677	62758	71686	77678	
5851	77679	62759	71687	77680	
5852	77681	62760	71688	77682	
5853	77683	62761	71689	77684	
5854	77685	62762	71690	77686	
5855	77687	62763	71691	77688	
5856	77689	62764	71692	77690	
5857	77691	62765	71693	77692	
5858	77693	62766	71694	77694	
5859	77695	62767	71695	77696	
5860	77697	62768	71696	77698	
5861	77699	62769	71697	77700	
5862	77701	62770	71698	77702	
5863	77703	62771	71699	77704	
5864	77705	62772	71700	77706	
5865	77707	62773	71701	77708	
5866	77709	62774	71702	77710	
5867	77711	62775	71703	77712	
5868	77713	62776	71704	77714	Repainted into retro BR blue/grey livery 2024 and displayed at the Greatest Gathering August 2025
5869	77715	62777	71705	77716	
5870	77717	62778	71706	77718	
5871	77719	62779	71707	77720	Preserved by Southern Electric Traction Group ion February 2026; named *Roy Watts MBE*
5872	77721	62780	71708	77722	
5873	77723	62781	71709	77724	
5874	77727	62782	71710	77726	

Opposite: **Although all the units were originally scheduled to have been withdrawn by the end of December 2025, South Western Railway retained a number of units to provide cover for the replacement Class 701s. On 3 March 2026 Nos 5712 and 5732 – both of which looked in excellent external condition – were utilised on the 09.03 service from Waterloo to Guildford via Cobham, which is seen here approaching its destination.** *Alex Dasi-Sutton*

Number	DMSO	MSO	TSO	DTSO	
5901	77813	62826	71714	77814	On 7 July 2017 at Guildford a faulty capacitor, installed as part of the electrical equipment update caused an explosion in an underframe equipment case
5902	77815	62827	71715	77816	
5903	77817	62828	71716	77818	
5904	77819	62829	71717	77820	
5905	77821	62830	71718	77822	
5906	77823	62831	71719	77824	
5907	77825	62832	71720	77826	
5908	77827	62833	71721	77828	
5909	77829	62834	71722	77830	
5910	77831	62835	71723	77832	
5911	77833	62836	71724	77834	
5912	77835	62837	71725	77836	71725 was replaced by TSO No 67400 (ex-60400 from Class 210 No 210002)
5913	77837	62838	71726	77838	62838 was scrapped following an incident on 5 November 2010 when a concrete mixer fell onto the 15.05 Guildford to London waterloo service; it was replaced by No 67301 (formerly DTSO No 60301 from Class 2120 No 210001) following rebuilding at Wolverton Works and incorporating the undamaged end of No 62838 to replace its existing driver's cab end.
5914	77839	62839	71727	77840	
5915	77841	62840	71728	77842	
5916	77843	62841	71729	77844	
5917	77845	62842	71730	77846	
5918	77847	62843	71731	77848	
5919	77849	62844	71732	77850	
5920	77851	62845	71733	77852	

The Brighton & Dyke Railway

Sited to the north-west of Brighton, the Devil's Dyke is a popular location situated on the South Downs. Although it was bypassed by the LBSCR route heading west from Brighton, there were proposals to provide a connection to the beauty spot.

Powers to construct the line from a junction, just to the west of West Brighton (later Hove) station, were first granted to the independent Brighton & Dyke Railway by an Act that received the Royal Assent on 2 August 1877. The newly approved railway's share capital was authorised as £72,000. However, opposition from the LBSCR and other factors delayed construction and these initial powers were allowed to lapse. However, a further Act, which received the Royal Assent on 18 July 1881, revived the project but the promoters sought and obtained time extensions for its construction and it was not until 1 September 1887 that the 3½-mile long single-track branch finally opened to a terminus at Hangleton; a mile-long section through to Poynings was never completed. The line, which was operated from its opening by the LBSCR, was steeply graded – at times 1 in 40 – as it had to climb some 400ft over the distance as well as having severe curves of 13 to 30 chain radius.

The first intermediate station on the line to be opened was Golf Club Halt; this was situated a short distance south of the terminus and was provided for users of the adjacent golf course. The halt – which was never in the public timetable – opened during 1891.

The line was never a great financial success; indeed, an official receiver was appointed in October 1895 although operation was maintained. In 1904, in order to improve the line's finances, the LBSCR replaced the existing rolling stock with a steam railmotor. Although its introduction allowed for an increase in frequency of the service – from the four return workings per day (including Sundays) that had operated prior to the introduction of the railmotor – the limited capacity of the stock – the locomotive was incapable of hauling a second carriage up the gradient – meant the trains were overcrowded.

Following the introduction of steam-hauled motor trains to the branch, two new halts were opened on the main line. Pictured at one of these – Dyke Junction – is 'Terrier' No 79 _Minories_. New in July 1880 and rebuilt in January 1912, the locomotive – latterly renumbered 679 – was sold to the Admiralty in January 1918 and was used at Catterick Camp and Chatham Dockyard before being scrapped in October 1933. _Crécy Archive_

There were also complaints about vibration, the sharp curves of the line would not have helped this, and of cleanliness. Following the introduction of the railmotors, the LBSCR opened Holland Road Halt and Dyke Junction Halt, both situated on the main line to Shoreham, on 3 September 1905.

In the late 19th century, there were efforts to increase the attractiveness of the Devil's Dyke; a fun fair and hotel were established at the summit and, in order to access this from the railway's terminus a funicular was constructed in 1897 to provide a link through to the summit. This 3ft 0in gauge line extended over a distance of some 840ft with gradients between 1 in 1½ and 1 in 3. Initially popular, the line was also mired in financial problems; put up for sale in December 1900 – albeit not being sold – it soldiered on until final closure came in 1908. There was also a cableway that crossed over the Dyke ravine; this 1,100ft long system was opened in 1894 and closed 15 years later.

Passenger services over the Brighton & Dyke Railway were suspended as a wartime measure on 1 January 1917; they were

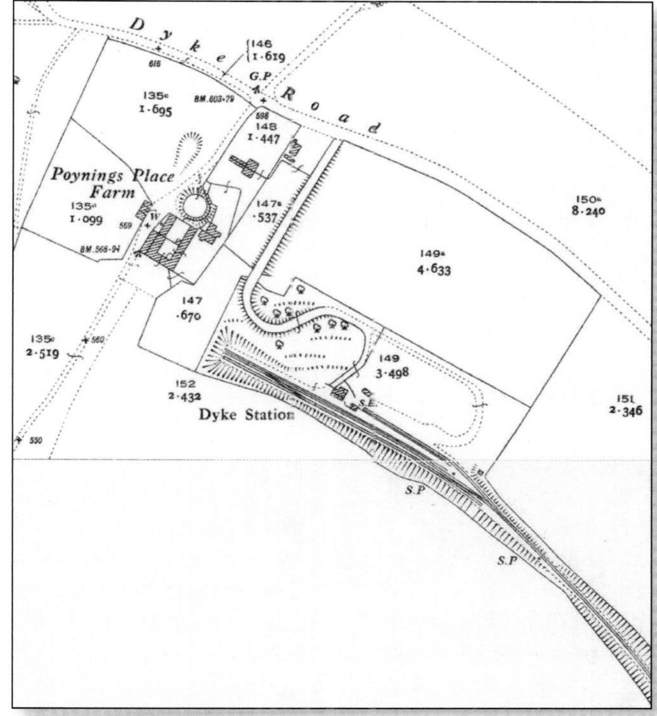

The terminus at The Dyke in 1931. Although primarily a passenger line for visitors to the Devil's Dyke, the station did have limited freight facilities. The traffic received was merchandise such as domestic coal; the very limited outbound traffic largely comprised occasional bales of hay.
Reproduced with the permission of National Library of Scotland

not to be reinstated until 26 July 1920. By this date the line's independent existence was drawing to a close. Although not initially incorporated by the Southern at Grouping, the line was subsumed on 22 July 1924.

In 1932 the SR introduced a new steam-powered railbus acquired from Sentinel-Cammell. This was fitted with wooden wheel centres in order to reduce noise – another of the complaints from passengers – but this adversely affected the track circuits when used on the main line. The railbus, successful in operation but lacking capacity, was to survive on the line for two years before being transferred to the Westerham branch; it was finally withdrawn in 1940 having seen operation on a number of other lines.

In later years the steam railmotor services generally terminated at Rowan Halt – a new station opened by the Southern on 18 December 1933 to serve new housing developments – with services to The Dyke generally hauled by a Class E4 0-6-2T. By the 1930s, the growth of competition from buses and private motor cars was proving increasing difficult to counter; the position of the railway was not aided by the fact

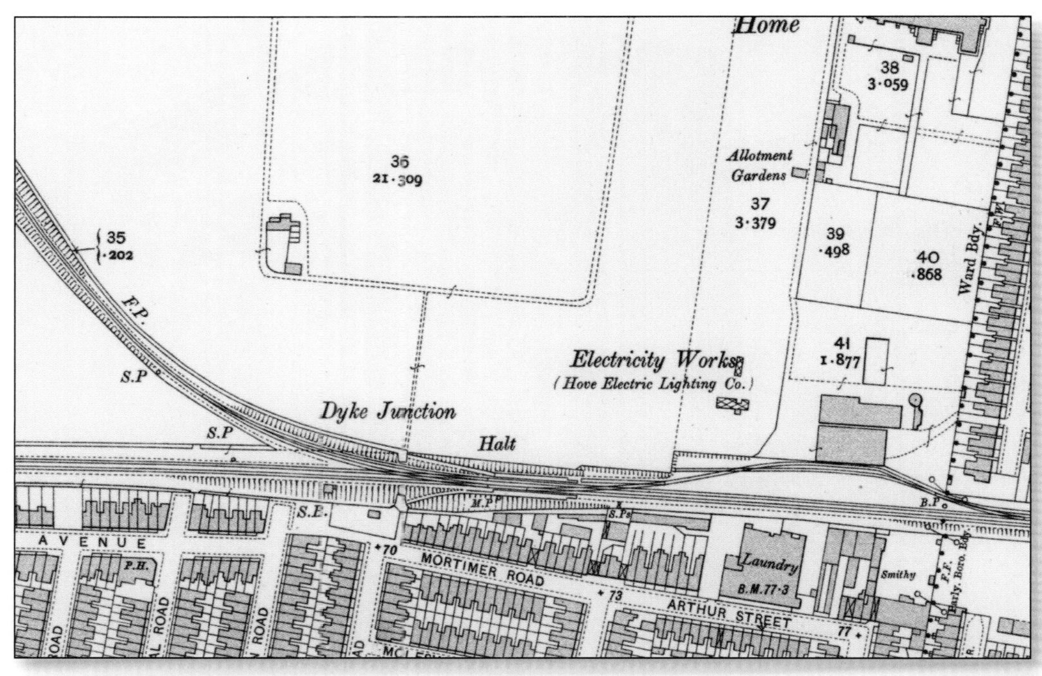

The branch headed north from the Brighton to Shoreham main line at Aldrington. When the line opened there was no provision for a station at the junction itself but the introduction of the steam railmotors in 1904 resulted in the LBSCR constructing a new station. Dyke Junction opened in September 1905; the station was renamed Aldrington Halt on 17 June 1932; the suffix 'Halt' was dropped on 5 May 1969.
Reproduced with the permission of the National Library of Scotland

BRIGHTON and THE DYKE (Motor Cars—One class only).—L. B. and S. C.

Miles		a	mrn	mrn	aft	aft	Except Sats. aft	Sats. aft	aft	aft	mrn	mrn	aft	aft	aft	aft
											Sundays					
	Central Station, Brighton ¶ ....dep.	10 0	11 3	1158	1250	1 45	2 35	2 40	4 40	5 50	10 0	1115	2 40	3 35	4 30	6 25
1¼	Hove ¶	10 9	11 9	12 4	1256	1 51	2 41	2 46	4 46	5 56	10 6	1121	2 46	3 41	4 36	6 31
5¼	The Dyke ....arr.	1025	1123	1218	1 10	2 5	2 55	3 0	5 0	6 10	1020	1135	3 0	3 55	4 50	6 45

Miles		a	mrn	aft	aft	aft	aft	aft	aft	mrn	aft	aft	aft	aft	aft
		Week Days								*Sundays*					
	The Dyke ¶ ....dep.	1045	1128	1225	1 20	2 10	4 15	5 10	6 15	1030	1 5	3 5	4 0	5 15	7 0
4	Hove ¶	11 1	1141	1238	1 33	2 23	4 28	5 23	6 28	1043	1 18	3 18	4 13	5 28	7 13
5¼	Brighton (C.) ..arr.	11 6	1147	1244	1 39	2 29	4 34	5 29	6 34	1049	1 24	3 24	4 19	5 31	7 19

a 1, 2, and 3 class Trains; not stopping at the Halts.

¶ "Halts" at Holland Road, between Brighton and Hove; and Dyke Junction, between Hove and The Dyke,

The timetable for the branch in April 1910 by which stage the steam railmotors had taken over the service. Of the two halts on the main line, Dyke Junction Halt was renamed Aldrington Halt on 17 June 1932 but Holland Road Halt was closed on 7 May 1956.

that these types of vehicle could easily transport the visitors to the summit whilst those arriving by train were faced by a wearying climb of some 200ft. It was, therefore, not a surprise when the line was closed completely on 31 December 1938.

The *Railway Magazine* of March 1939 recorded the demise of the line in detail. The final Down train – which departed from Brighton at 5.7pm – was hauled by Class E4 No 2505 and comprised the usual 'Balloon' coach, which had been reserved by local enthusiasts that evening, supplemented by a rake of three ex-SECR coaches. One of the doors on the reserved coach carried a board that portrayed a caricature of an elderly train allied to the legend: 'Born 1887. So Long, Old Timer!' The author of the tribute, Frank S. White, described the final ascent of the gradient in glowing terms: 'At Aldrington the main line was left and after one more stop at Rowan Halt, No. 2505 applied herself to the serious task of climbing nearly three miles of steep, twisting gradients. Now it became unwise to put one's head out of the window; the tank, hard at work, was celebrating the occasion in her own way with a lavish display of fireworks, and red-hot cinders were falling all around. Upwards she plugged, speed dropping to somewhere about 12mph till presently appeared the green light of the Dyke home signal, lowered probably for the last time.' The train departed to the inevitable cacophony of detonators for its return to Brighton; White signed off the piece: 'The Old Year was dying; the Dyke branch was dead'.

Pictured awaiting disposal at Ashford Works in a derelict condition on 20 September 1947 is the unique Southern Railway lightweight Sentinel-Cammell steam railmotor No 6. The design of the unit was approved by Richard Maunsell. It was designed for, effectively, one-man operation in that the branch was short enough to be operated for one return trip on a single firing with the firebox stoked up before departure. *Peter N. Williams/Online Transport Archive*

Right: **The Victorian businessman James Henry Hubbard created an amusement park at Devil's Dyke; this was, however, at some distance from the terminus of the LBSCR station. In order to provide a link between the two, he commissioned Charles O. Blaber, who had previously been the engineer responsible for constructing the Brighton & Dyke Railway, to design a funicular – the Steep Grade Railway – to link the two. Constructed in six months, the line, which was 840ft in length and built to the 3ft 0in gauge, opened in July 1897. The line climbed to a height of 395ft; at the lower level, there was no building but a simple brick platform with buffers.** *Barry Cross Collection/Online Transport Archiver*

Above: **The provision at the upper level of the Steep Grade Railway was slightly more substantial and incorporated a brick-built structure that acted both as a station and as the engine house for the line. The power for the line was provided by a water-cooled 25hp Hornsby Ackroyd oil engine. Two open 12-seat carriages were provided; the basic livery was red. The Steep Grade Railway was initially successful financially but by 1899 it was in financial difficulty and operations were temporarily withdrawn. Sold in 1900 at auction, services were reinstated; however, by the end of the decade the line had again closed, this time permanently. The line was dismantled in about 1913.**
John Meredith Collection/Online Transport Archive

Right: **The funicular was not the only additional form of transport that Hubbard developed to exploit his investments at Devil's Dyke. This was the 1,100ft cableway that crossed the Dyke ravine completed in 1894.**
John Meredith Collection/Online Transport Archive

SOUTHERN STATIONS 8
KENT SOUTH
Paul Smith

PLEASE NOTE THAT THE SCALES OF THE MAPS VARY AND ARE FOR ILLUSTRATIVE PURPOSES

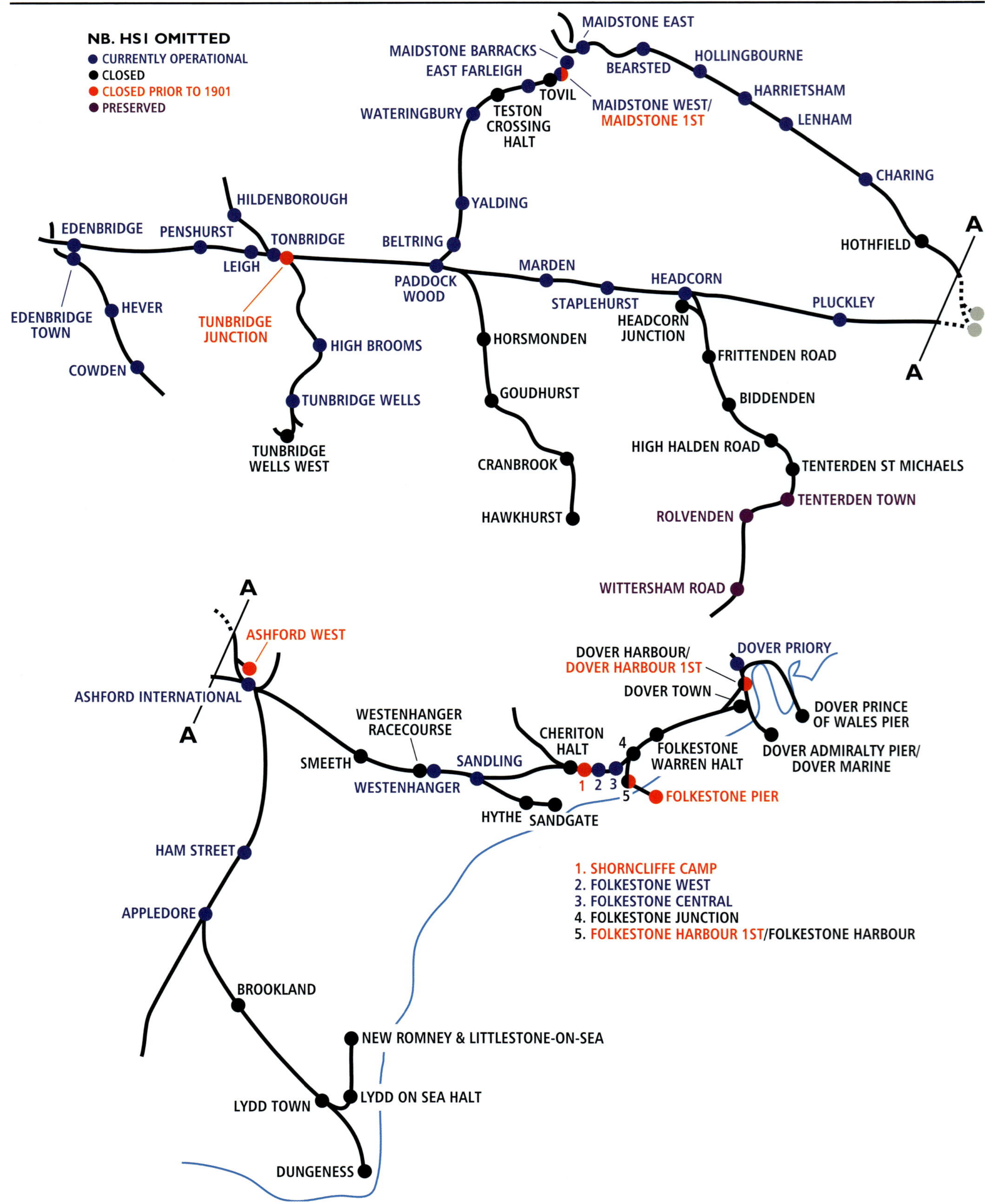

APPLEDORE

Opened 13 February 1851 by the SER.
TQ97568 29761

ASHFORD INTERNATIONAL

Opened 1 December 1942 by the SER as *Ashford*, renamed as *Ashford (Kent)* 9 July 1923 by the SR and as *Ashford International* 8 January 1996 by BR.

ASHFORD WEST

Opened 1 July 1884 by the LC&DR and closed 1 January 1899.
Line lifted – Demolished – HS1 passes through the station

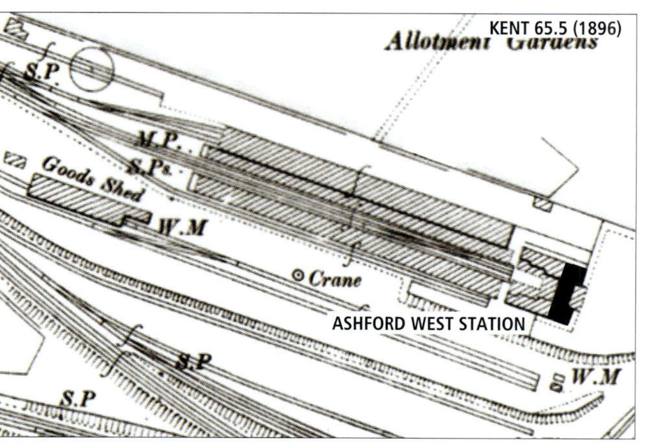

BEARSTED

Opened 1 July 1884 by the LC&DR as *Bearsted*, renamed as *Eearsted & Thurnham* 1 July 1907 and reverted to *Bearsted* 12 May 1980 by BR.   **TQ79868 56135**

BELTRING

Cpened 1 September 1909 by the SE&CR as *Beltring and Banbridges Halt* and renamed as *Beltring* 12 May 1980 by BR.   **TQ67995 47803**

BIDDENDEN

Opened 15 May 1905 by the Kent & East Sussex Railway and closed 4 January 1954 by BR.
Line lifted - Station building and platforms in private use
TQ85308 39217

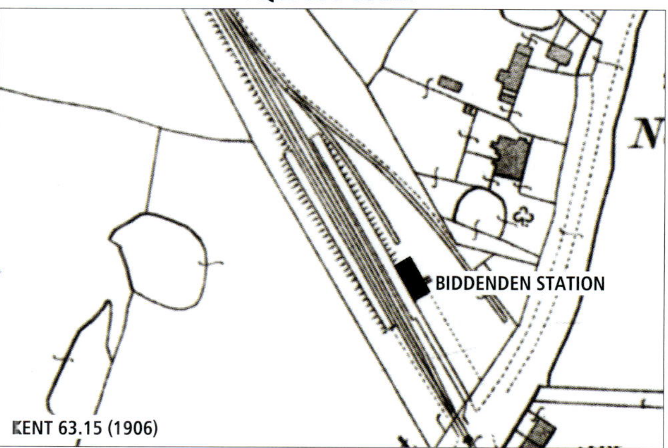

BROOKLAND

Opened 7 December 1881 by the Lydd Railway as *Brookland*, renamed as *Brookland Halt* c1923 by the SR, as *Brookland* c1934, as *Brookland Halt* in 1954 by BR and closed 6 March 1967.

Line Operational for Freight - Station building and platform in private use **TQ99724 26403**

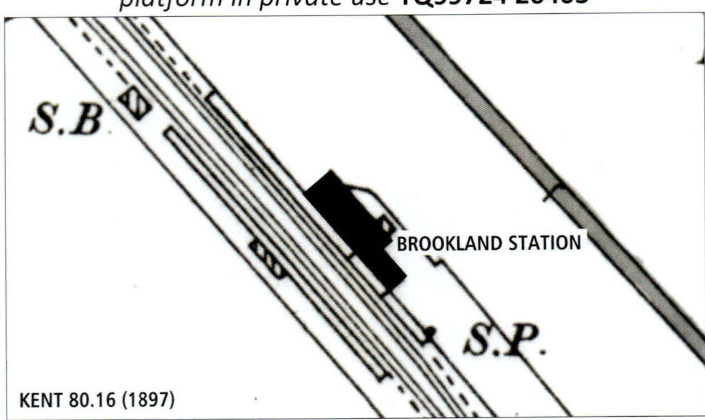

CHARING

Opened 1 July 1884 by the Maidstone & Ashford Railway.
TQ94994 49132

CHERITON HALT

Opened 1 May 1908 by the SE&CR, closed 1 December 1915, reopened 14 June 1920, closed 1 February 1941 by the SR, reopened 7 October 1946 and finally closed 16 June 1947.

Line Operational – Demolished – No access
TR20113 36612

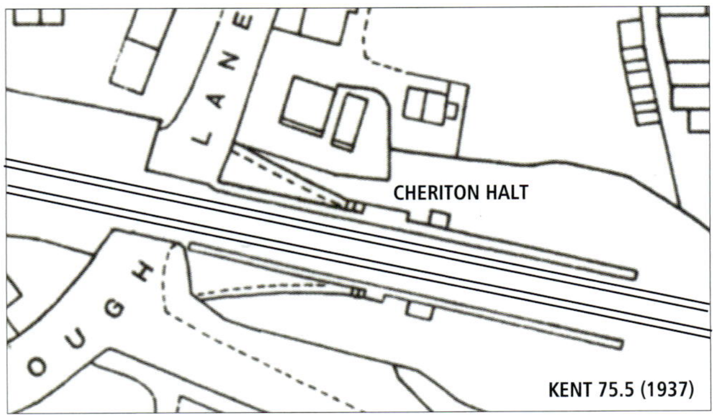

COWDEN

Opened 1 October 1888 by the LB&SCR.
TQ47657 41714

CRANBROOK

Opened 4 September 1893 by the Cranbrook & Paddock Wood Railway and closed 12 June 1961 by BR.

Line lifted – Station site and building in commercial use – Station Master's House in private use **TQ75339 34509**

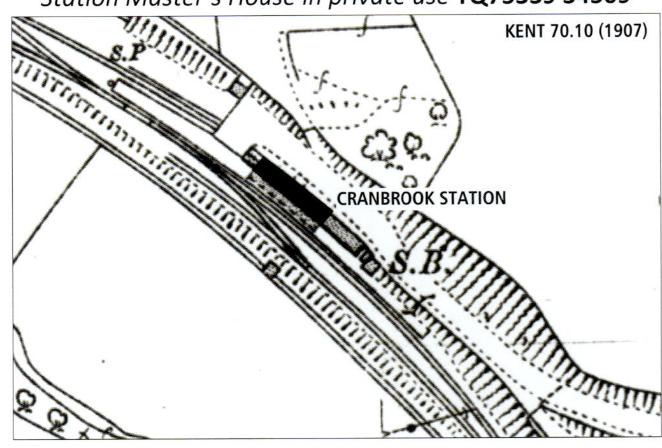

DOVER ADMIRALTY PIER

Opened 30 August 1864 by the SER and closed in August 1914 by the SE&CR.

Line lifted - Demolished **TR32052 40098 (a)**

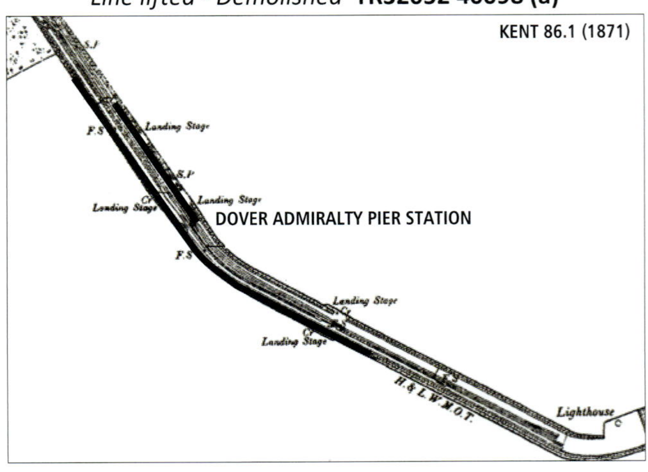

DOVER HARBOUR (1st)

Opened 1 November 1861 by the LC&DR and closed in June 1863.
Line Operational – Demolished **TR31644 40549 (a)**

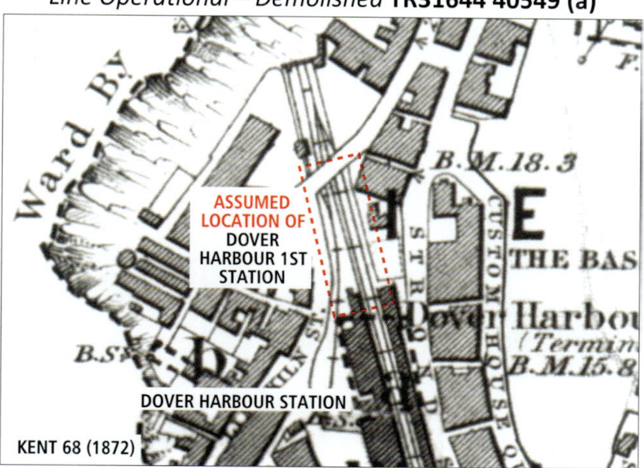

DOVER HARBOUR

Opened in June 1863 by the LC&DR as *Dover Town & Harbour*, renamed as *Dover Harbour* 1 June 1899 by the SE&CR and closed 10 July 1927 by the SR.
Line Operational - Station building in commercial use - Platforms demolished **TR31644 40549**

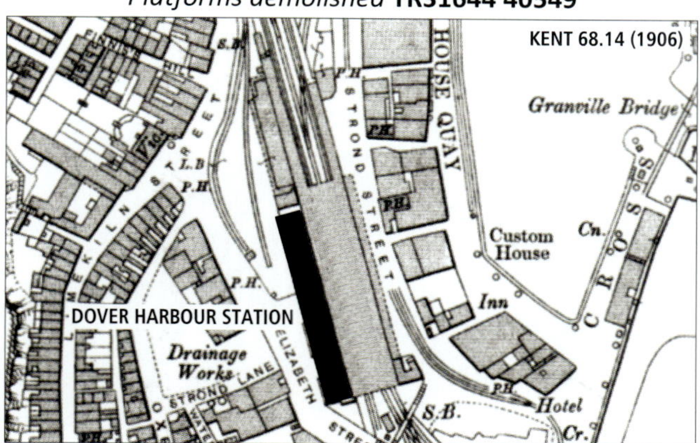

DOVER MARINE

Opened 2 February 1915 by the SE&CR as *Dover Admiralty Pier*, renamed as *Dover Marine* 5 December 1918, as *Dover Western Docks* in 1979 by BR and closed 25 September 1994.
Line lifted – Grade II listed building in use as a cruise terminal **TR32125 40138**

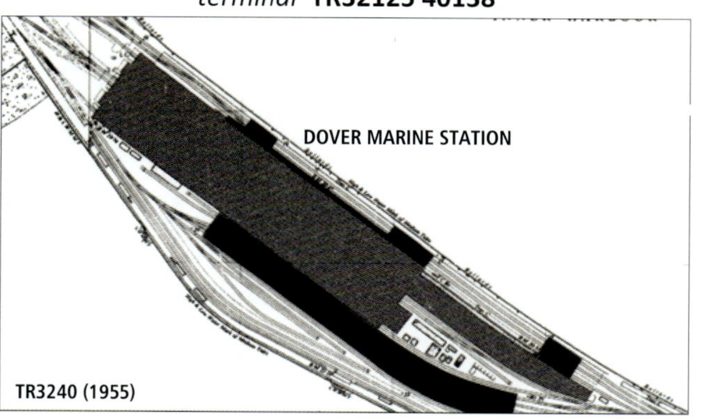

DOVER PRINCE OF WALES PIER

Opened in 1903 by the SE&CR and closed in 1914.
Line lifted – Platforms demolished **TR32566 40332**

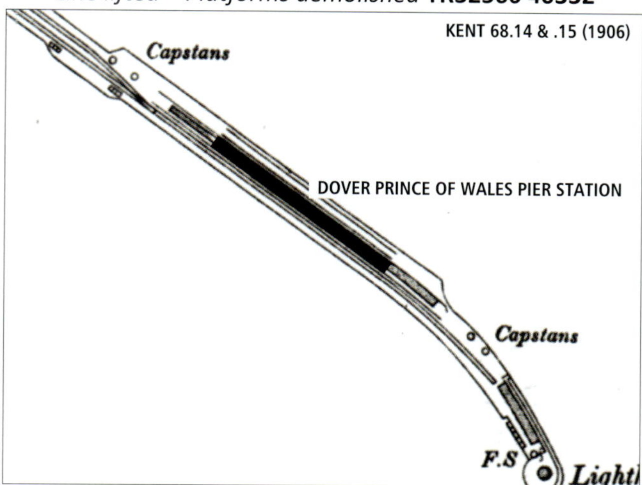

DOVER PRIORY

Opened 22 July 1861 by the LC&DR as *Dover Town (Priory)* and renamed as *Dover Priory* in 1863.
TR31342 41509

DOVER TOWN

Opened 7 February 1844 by the SER as *Dover*, renamed as *Dover Town* in December 1861 and closed 14 October 1914.
Line lifted – Demolished – Station site occupied by a lorry park **TR31771 40289**

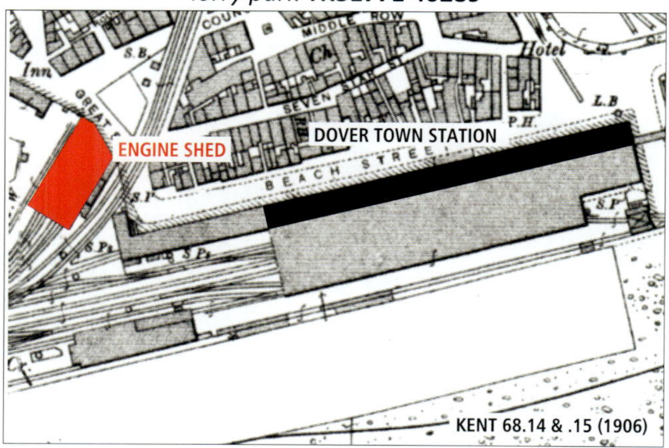

DUNGENESS

Opened 1 April 1883 by the Lydd Railway and closed 4 July 1937 by the SR.
Line lifted – Demolished - Platforms partially extant and base of station building remains **TR08809 17037**

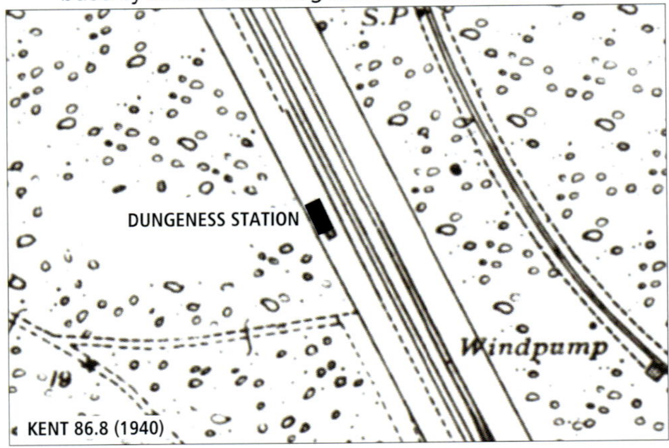

EAST FARLEIGH

Opened 25 September 1844 by the SER.
TQ73498 53620

EDENBRIDGE

Opened 26 May 1842 by the SER.
TQ43998 47477

EDENBRIDGE TOWN

Opened 2 January 1888 by the LB&SCR as *Edenbridge* and renamed as *Edenbridge Town* 1 May 1896.
TQ44552 46558

FOLKESTONE CENTRAL

Opened 18 August 1884 by the SER as *Cheriton Arch*, renamed as *Radnor Park* in 1886 and as *Folkestone Central* 1 June 1895.   **TR22018 36276**

FOLKESTONE HARBOUR (1st)

Opened 1 January 1849 by the SER and closed 16 August 1861.
Line Operational – Demolished **TR23341 35839**

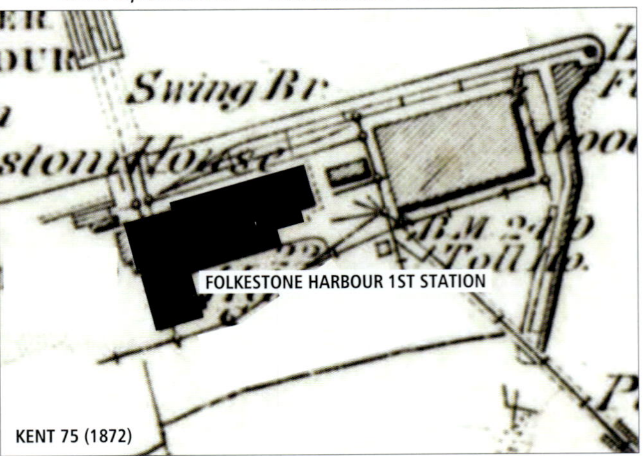

FOLKESTONE HARBOUR

Opened 16 August 1861 by the SER, closed in April 1916 by the SE&CR, reopened 3 February 1919, closed 4 January 1995 by BR, reopened 31 March 1995 and finally closed to regular passenger traffic 2 October 2000.
Line lifted - Partially demolished - Platforms, canopies and some buildings have been refurbished - A pathway passes through the site **TR23434 35778**

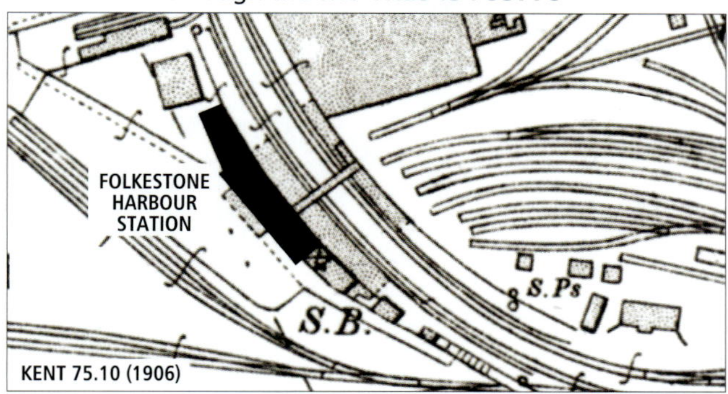

FOLKESTONE JUNCTION

Opened 18 December 1843 by the SER as *Folkestone* renamed as *Folkestone Old* in July 1849, as *Folkestone Junction* in January 1852, as *Folkestone Junction (Shorncliffe)* in September 1858, as *Folkestone Junction* in November 1863, as *Folkestone* in April 1884, as *Folkestone Junction* in June 1897, as *Folkestone East* 10 September 1962 by BR and closed 6 September 1965.

Line Operational – Demolished - Up platform and part of the Down platform are extant and used by railway staff

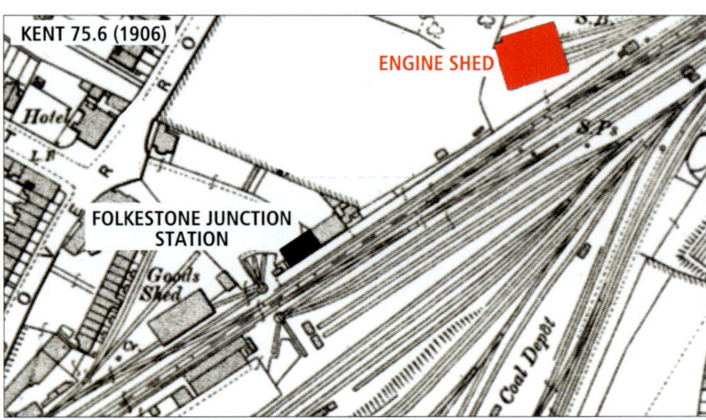

FOLKESTONE PIER

Opened 4 March 1876 by the SER and closed in 1883.
Line lifted – Demolished – Station site in dockyard use
TR23623 35668

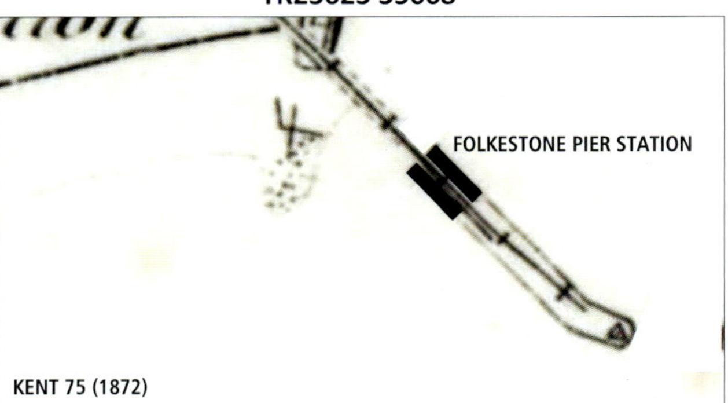

FOLKESTONE WARREN HALT

Opened c1884 by the SER as *Folkestone Warren*, closed 29 September 1888, reopened as *Folkestone Warren Halt* 1 June 1908 by the SE&CR, closed 19 December 1915, reopened 30 July 1923 by the SR, closed 1 December 1940, reopened in 1946 and closed c1957 by BR.
Line Operational – Eastbound platform extant – No access
TR24835 37849

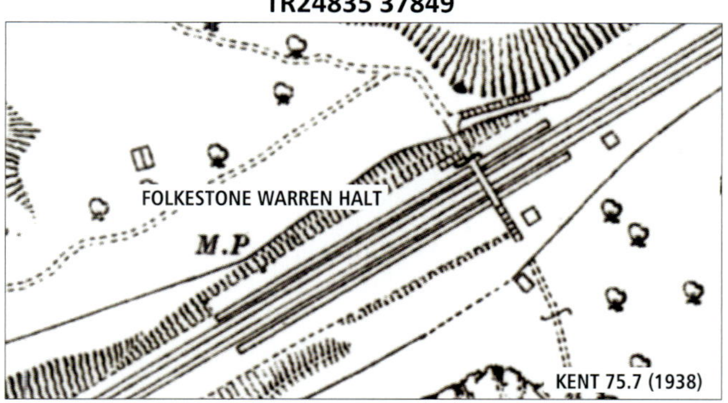

FOLKESTONE WEST

Opened 1 February 1881 by the SER as *Shorncliffe Camp*, renamed as *Shorncliffe* 2 July 1926 by the SR and as *Folkestone West* 10 September 1962.
TR20988 36445

FRITTENDEN ROAD

Opened 15 May 1905 by the Kent & East Sussex Railway and closed 4 January 1954 by BR.
Line lifted – Demolished – Station site in commercial use as "The Old Frittenden Road Station" **TQ84271 40833**

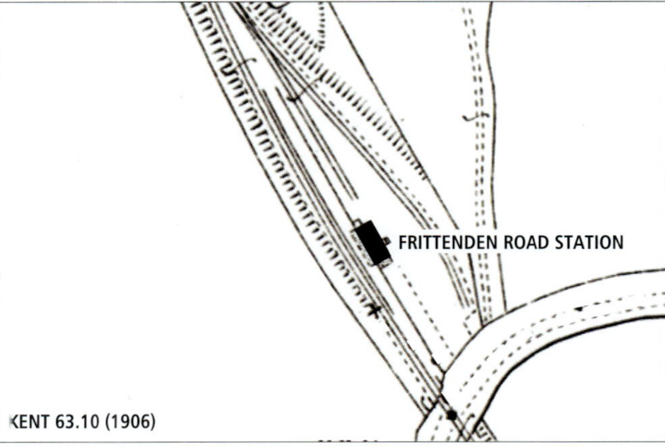

GOUDHURST

Opened 12 September 1892 by the Cranbrook & Paddock Wood Railway as *Hope Mill for Goudhurst and Lamberhurst*, renamed as *Goudhurst* 1 December 1892 by the SER and closed 12 June 1961 by BR.
Line lifted – Demolished - Station site occupied by a private dwelling **TQ70860 37262**

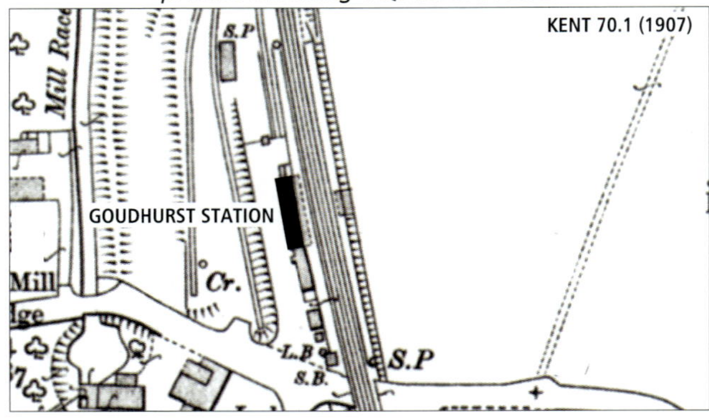

HAWKHURST

Opened 4 September 1893 by the Cranbrook & Paddock Wood Railway and closed 12 June 1961 by BR.
Line lifted – Demolished - Station site in commercial use as the "Hawkhurst Station Business Park" **TQ75685 32278**

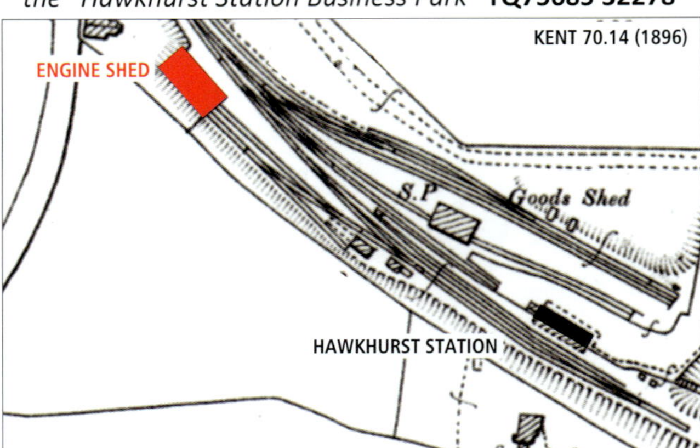

HAM STREET

Opened 13 February 1851 by the SER as *Ham Street*, renamed as *Ham Street & Orlestone* 1 February 1897 and reverted to *Ham Street* 3 May 1976 by BR.
TR00100 33756

HEADCORN

Opened 31 August 1842 by the SER.
TQ83755 43996

HARRIETSHAM

Opened 1 July 1884 by the Maidstone & Ashford Railway.
TQ86660 52915

HEADCORN JUNCTION

Opened 15 May 1905 by the Kent & East Sussex Railway and closed 4 January 1954 by BR.
Line Operational – Demolished – No access
TQ83704 43979

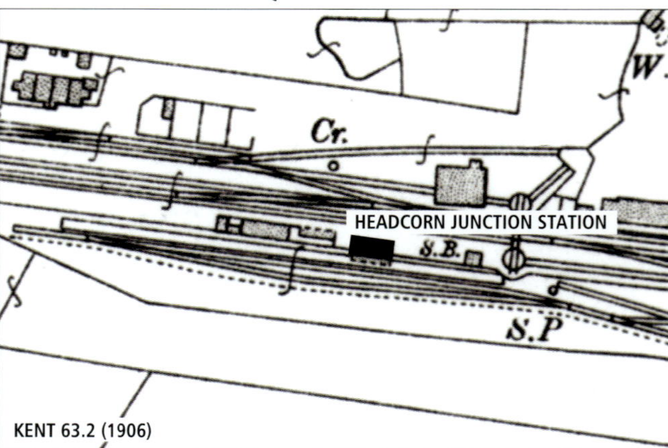

HEVER

Opened 1 October 1888 by the LB&SCR.
TQ46500 44559

HIGH BROOMS

Opened 1 March 1893 by the SER as *Southborough* and renamed as *High Brooms* 21 September 1925 by the SR.
TQ59431 41431

HIGH HALDEN ROAD

Opened 15 May 1905 by the Kent & East Sussex Railway and closed 4 January 1954 by BR.
Line lifted – Station building and platform in commercial use **TQ87738 36768**

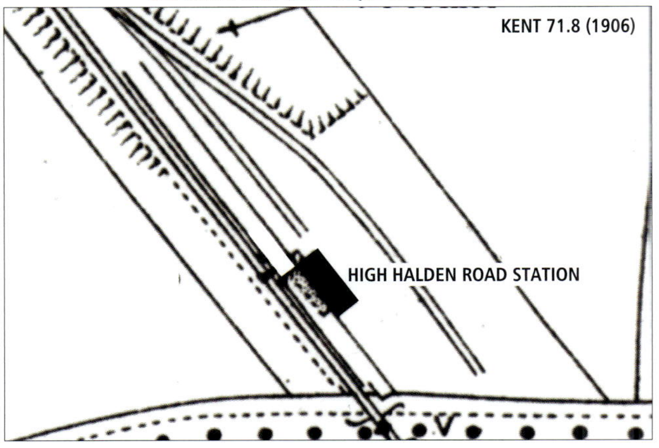

HILDENBOROUGH

Opened 1 May 1868 by the SER.
TQ55685 48518

HOLLINGBOURNE

Opened 1 July 1884 by the Maidstone & Ashford Railway.
TQ83421 55086

HORSMONDEN

Opened 12 September 1892 by the Cranbrook & Paddock Wood Railway and closed 12 June 1961 by BR.
Line lifted - Station building in commercial use as the "Old Station Garage" **TQ70556 40383**

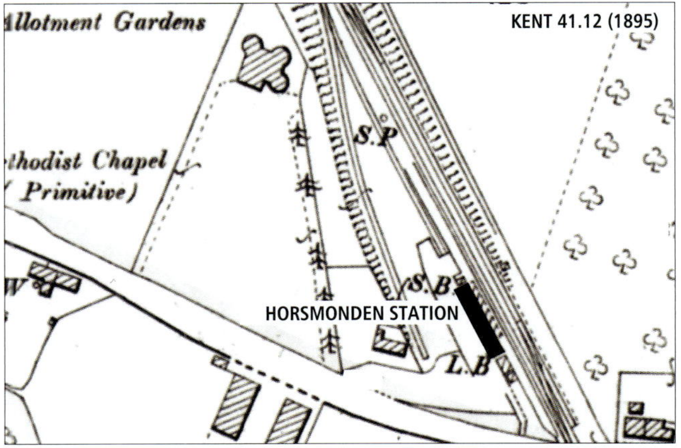

HOTHFIELD

Opened 1 July 1884 by the Maidstone & Ashford Railway as *Hothfield*, renamed as *Hothfield Halt* 13 August 1937 by the SR and closed 2 November 1959 by BR.
Line Operational – Demolished **TQ98075 46250**

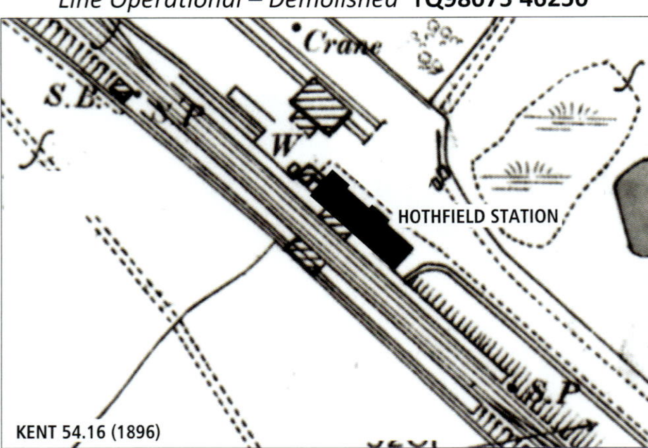

HYTHE

Opened 6 October 1874 by the SER as *Hythe*, renamed as *Hythe (Kent)* 21 September 1925 by the SR, as *Hythe for Sandgate* in November 1931, reverted to *Hythe* 5 July 1939 closed 3 May 1943, reopened 1 October 1945 and finally closed 3 December 1951 by BR.
Line lifted – Demolished – Station site occupied by housing in Cliffe Close **TR16799 35340**

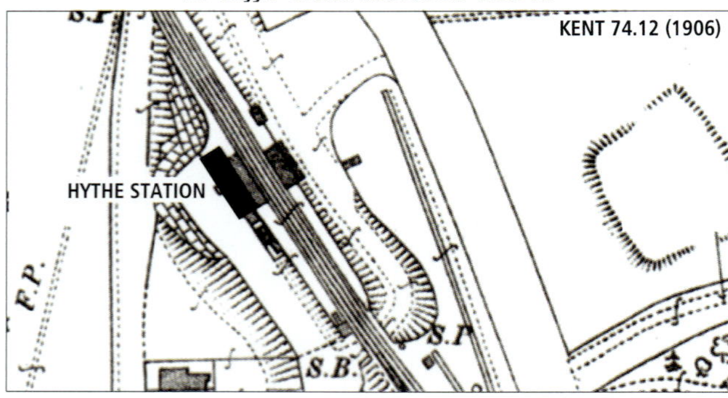

LEIGH

Opened 1 September 1911 by the SE&CR as *Leigh Halt* renamed as *Lyghe Halt* in April 1917, as *Leigh Halt* 13 June 1960 by BR and *as* Leigh 5 May 1969.
TQ54612 46186

LENHAM

Opened 1 July 1884 by the Maidstone & Ashford Railway.
TQ89139 51830

LYDD-ON-SEA HALT

Opened 4 July 1937 by the SR as *Lydd-on-Sea*, renamed as *Lydd-on-Sea Halt* 20 September 1954 by BR and closed 6 March 1967.
Line lifted – Demolished – Station site unused
TR08402 19080

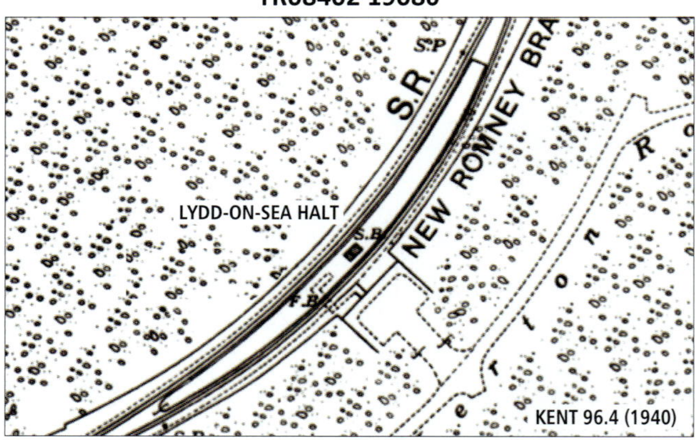

LYDD TOWN

Opened 7 December 1881 by the Lydd Railway as *Lydd*, renamed as *Lydd Town* 4 July 1937 by the SR and closed 6 March 1967 by BR.
Line Operational for Freight - Station building and platform extant and derelict **TR04980 21540**

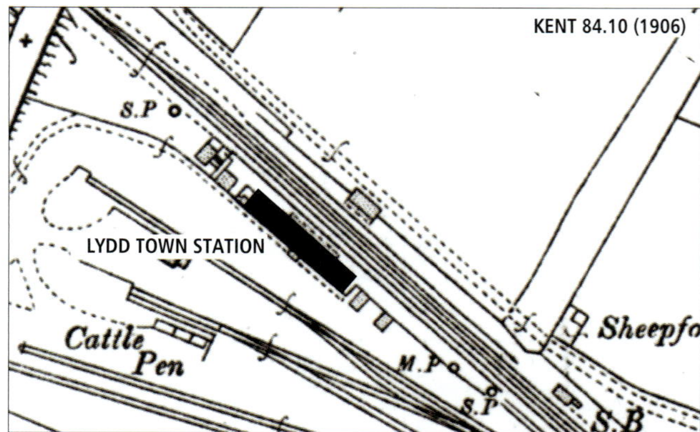

MAIDSTONE (lst)

Opened 25 September 1844 by the SER and closed in 1856.
Line lifted – Demolished – Station site in commercial use
TQ75646 55320

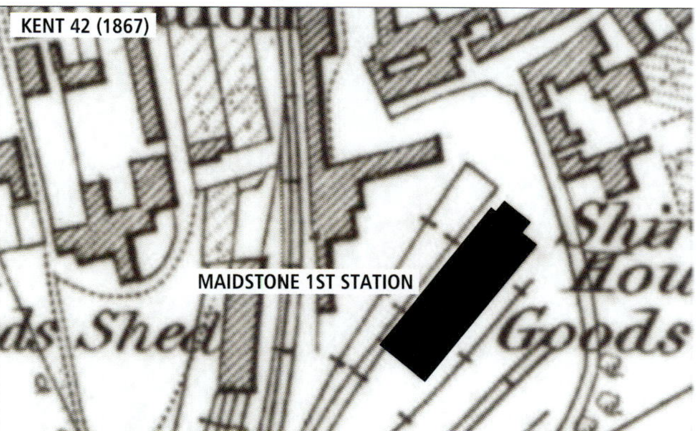

MAIDSTONE WEST

Opened in 1856 by the SER as *Maidstone* and renamed as *Maidstone West* 1 June 1899.
TQ75597 55348

MAIDSTONE BARRACKS

Opened 1 July 1874 by the SER.
TQ75460 56086

MARDEN

Opened 31 August 1842 by the SER.
TQ74450 44749

MAIDSTONE EAST

Opened 1 June 1874 by the Sevenoaks, Maidstone & Tonbridge Railway as *Maidstone* and renamed as *Maidstone East* 1 June 1899 by the LC&DR.
TQ75853 56170

NEW ROMNEY & LITTLESTONE-ON-SEA

Opened 19 June 1884 by the Lydd Railway as *New Romney & Littlestone*, renamed as *New Romney & Littlestone-on-Sea* in 1888 by the SER and closed 6 March 1967 by BR.
Line lifted – Demolished – Station site occupied by an industrial estate **TR07343 24751**

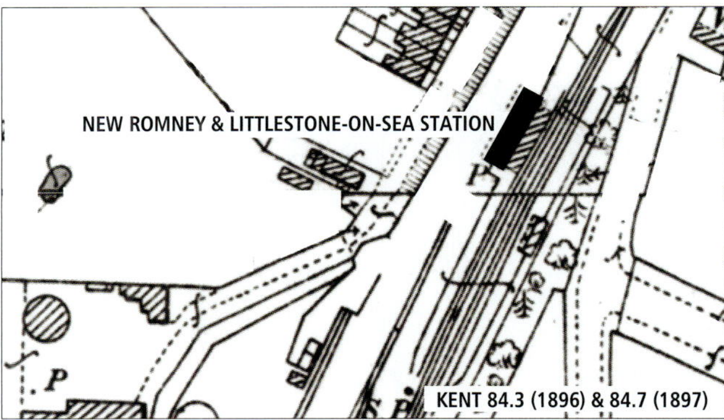

PADDOCK WOOD

Opened 31 August 1842 by the SER as *Maidstone Road* and renamed as *Paddock Wood* in 1844.
TQ67121 45284

PENSHURST

Opened 26 May 1842 by the SER.
TQ51948 46471

PLUCKLEY

Opened 1 December 1842 by the SER.
TQ92219 43275

ROLVENDEN

Opened 2 April 1900 by the Rother Valley Light Railway as *Tenterden*, renamed as *Rolvenden* 16 March 1903, closed 4 January 1954 by BR and reopened 3 February 1974 by the Kent & East Sussex Railway Preservation Society.
TQ86484 32769

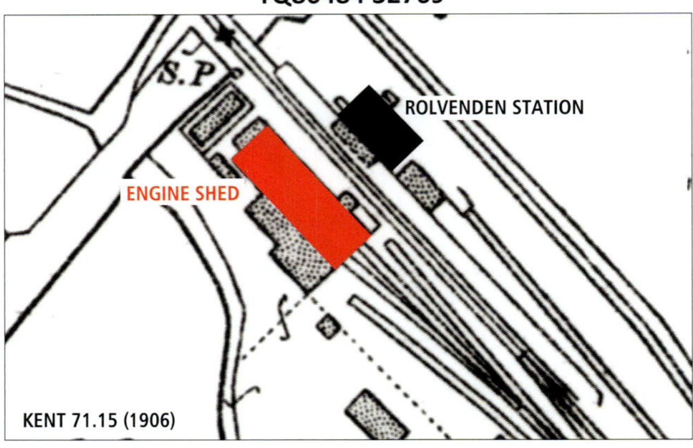

SANDGATE

Opened 6 October 1874 by the SER and closed 1 April 1931 by the SR.
Line lifted – Demolished – Station site occupied by housing in Battery Point **TR18854 35000**

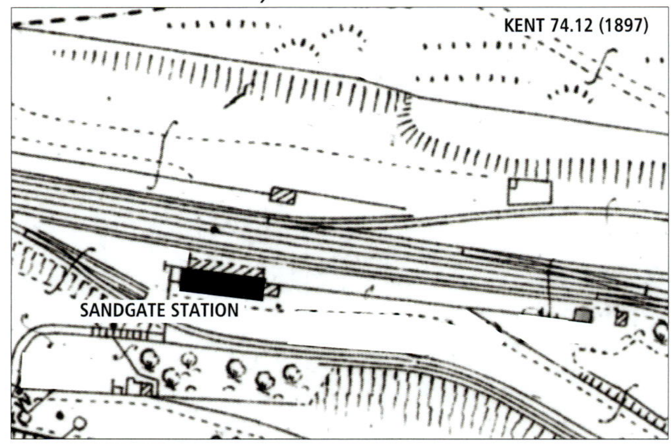

SANDLING

Opened 1 January 1888 by the SER as *Sandling Junction*, renamed as *Sandling for Hythe* 3 December 1951 by BR and as *Sandling* 12 May 1980.
TR14835 36827

SHORNCLIFFE CAMP

Opened 1 November 1863 by the SER as *Shorncliffe Camp*, renamed as *Shorncliffe & Sandgate* 1 December 1863, reverted to *Shorncliffe Camp* 1 October 1874 and closed 1 February 1881.

Line Operational – Demolished – No access
TR20755 36487

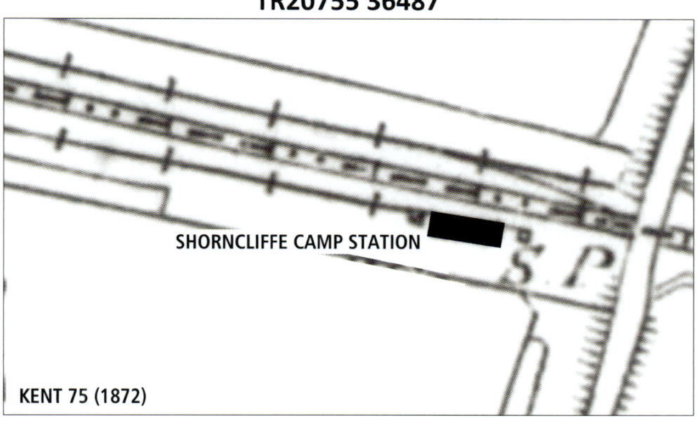

SMEETH

Opened in October 1852 by the SER and closed 4 January 1954 by BR.

Line Operational – Demolished **TR06864 38405**

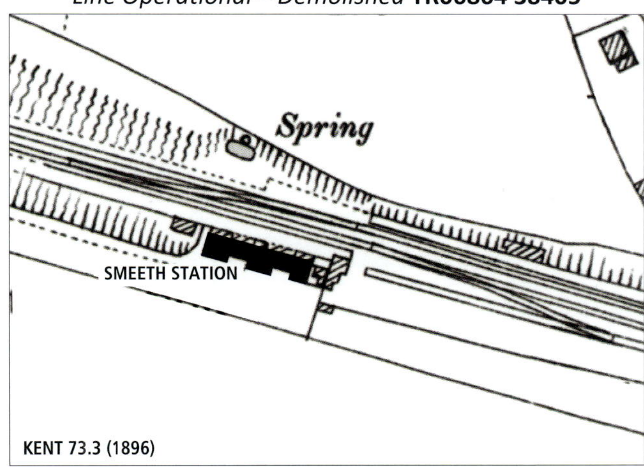

STAPLEHURST

Opened 31 August 1842 by the SER.
TQ78410 44456

TENTERDEN ST MICHAELS

Opened 1 May 1912 by the Kent & East Sussex Railway and closed 4 January 1954 by BR.

Line lifted – Demolished – A cycle/walkway passes through the station site **TQ88321 35185**

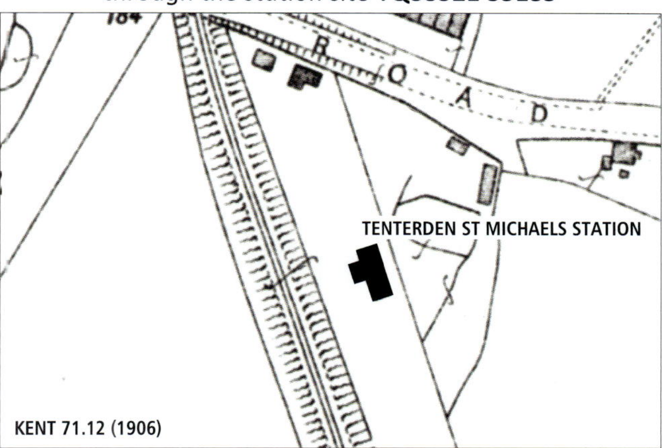

TENTERDEN TOWN

Opened 16 March 1903 by the Kent & East Sussex Railway, closed 4 January 1954 by BR and reopened 3 February 1974 by the Kent & East Sussex Railway Preservation Society.
TQ88225 33548

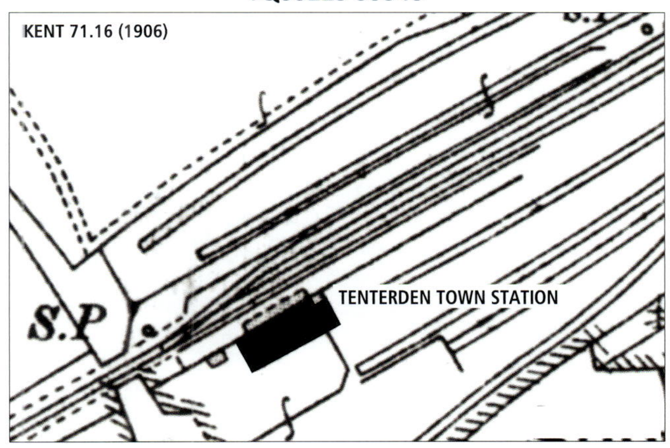

TESTON CROSSING HALT

Opened 1 September 1909 by the SE&CR and closed 2 November 1959 by BR.

Line Operational – Demolished **TQ70731 53350**

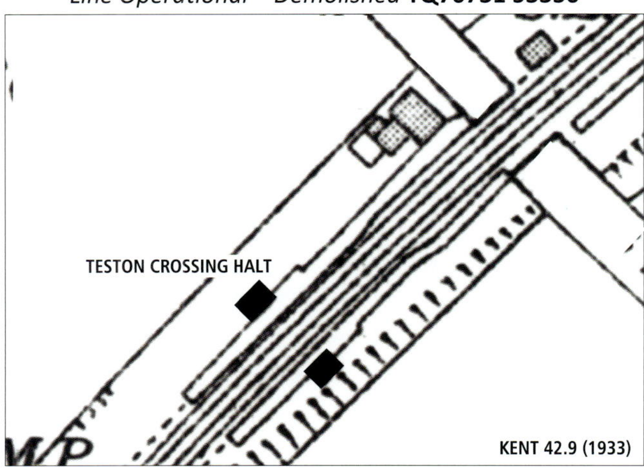

TONBRIDGE

Opened in 1864 by the SER as *Tunbridge Junction*, renamed as *Tonbridge Junction* in May 1893 and as *Tonbridge* 7 June 1929 by the SR.   **TQ58664 46046**

TUNBRIDGE WELLS

Opened 25 November 1846 by the SER as *Tunbridge Wells*, renamed as *Tunbridge Wells Central* 9 July 1923 by the SR and reverted to *Tunbridge Wells* 14 May 1979 by BR.
TQ58448 39168

TOVIL

Opened 1 January 1884 by the SER and closed 15 March 1943 by the SR.
Line Operational – Demolished – No access
TQ75197 54927

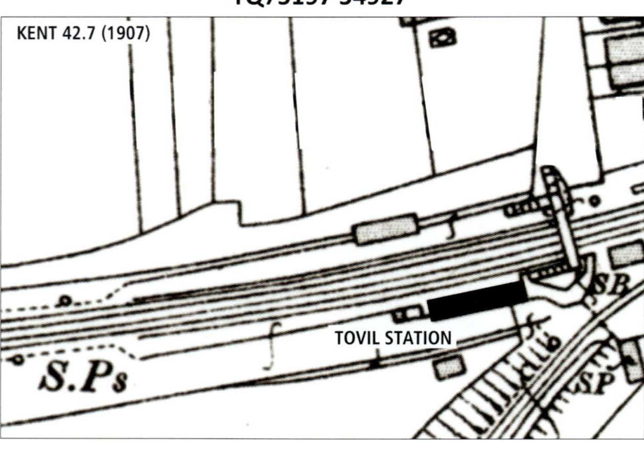

TUNBRIDGE WELLS WEST

Opened 1 October 1866 by the Brighton, Uckfield & Tunbridge Wells Railway as *Tunbridge Wells*, renamed as *Tunbridge Wells West* 22 August 1923 by the SR and closed 8 July 1985 by BR.
Line lifted - Station building and part of platform extant in use as the "Smith & Western" pub **TQ57871 38454**

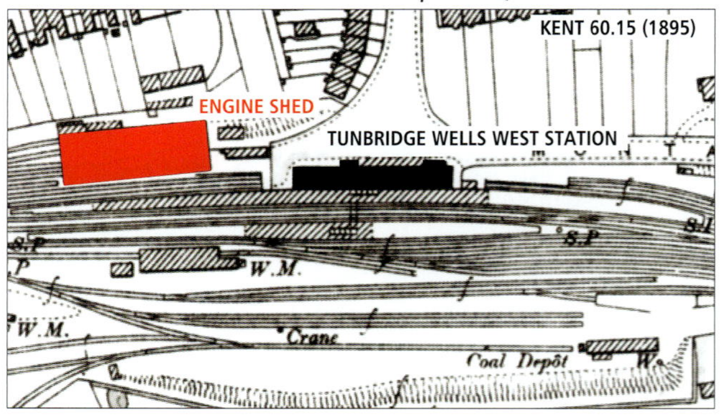

TUNBRIDGE JUNCTION (1st)

Opened 26 May 1842 by the SER as *Tunbridge*, renamed as *Tunbridge Junction* in 1852 and closed in 1864.
Line Operational – Demolished – No access
TQ59000 45990 (a)

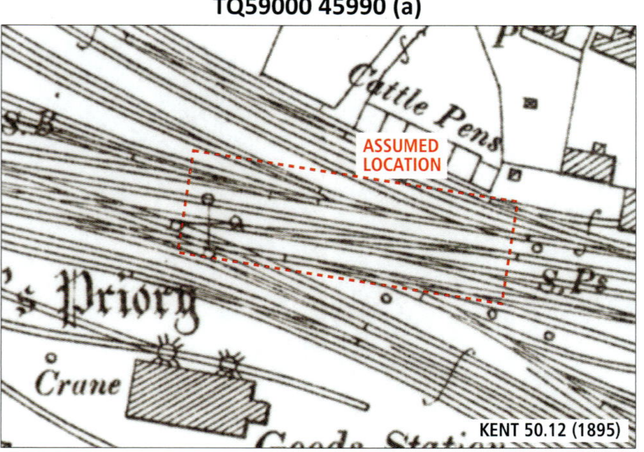

WATERINGBURY

Opened 25 September 1844 by the SER.
TQ69131 52830

WESTENHANGER

Opened 7 February 1844 by the SER as *Westenhanger*, renamed as *Westenhanger & Hythe* in 1846 and reverted to *Westenhanger* 1 October 1874.
TR12776 37253

WESTENHANGER RACECOURSE

Opened 30 March 1898 by the SER and closed in 1976 by BR.

Line Operational – Demolished **TR12519 37305**

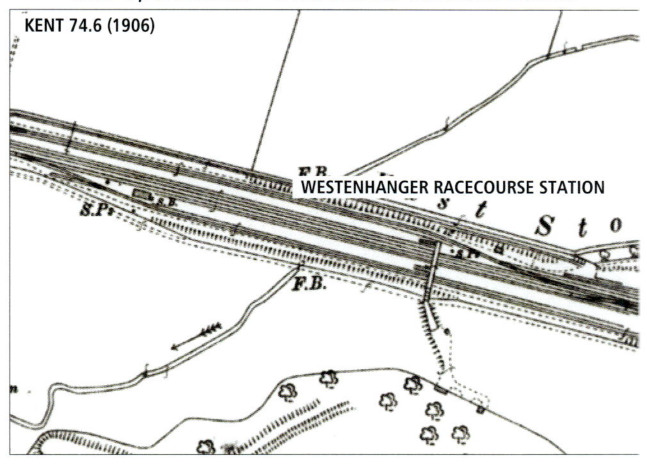

WITTERSHAM ROAD

Opened 2 April 1900 by the Rother Valley Light Railway, closed 4 January 1954 by BR and reopened 4 January 1977 by the Kent & East Sussex Railway Preservation Society.
TQ86688 28752

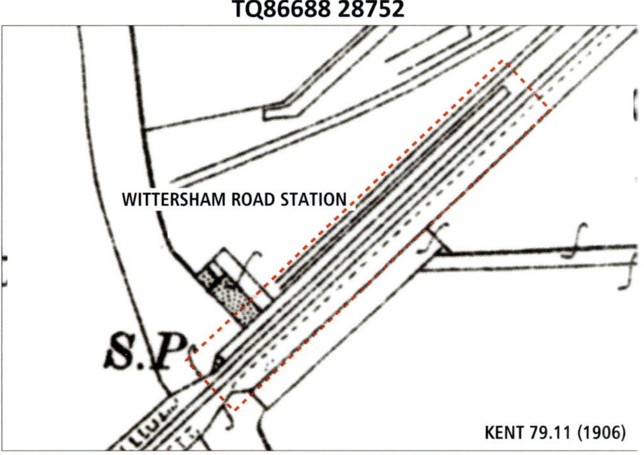

YALDING

Opened 25 September 1844 by the SER.
TQ68523 50255

BIBLIOGRAPHY

Railway Atlas Then and Now by Paul Smith & Keith Turner Crécy Publishing Third Edition (2020). ISBN 978-0-86093-698-5

Railway Passenger Stations in Great Britain: A Chronology by Michael Quick. Railway & Canal Historical Society (2009). ISBN 978-0-901461-57-5

The Directory of Railway Stations by RVJ Butt. Patrick Stephens Ltd (1995). ISBN 1-85260-508-1

British Railway Stations 1825-1900: An Essential Gazetteer by Paul Smith & Sally Salmon. Unique Books (2023) ISBN 978-1-913555-15-3

British Railway Stations Since 1901: An Essential Gazetteer by Paul Smith & Sally Salmon. Unique Books (2022) ISBN 978-1-913555-11-5

WEBSITES ACCESSED

Disused Stations: http://disused-stations.org.uk/
National Library of Scotland: www.nls.uk

Maps sourced from the Cambridge University Map Library are reproduced by permission of the Syndics of Cambridge University.

On 26 August 1959 Ivatt designed 2-6-2T No 41310 is seen at Ashford with the 3.35pm service from Maidstone East. *Alexander McBlain/Online Transport Archive*

Biddenden station, on the Kent & East Sussex, looking towards the north on 3 December 1953. *Neil Davenport/Online Transport Archive*

Cranbrook station viewed from the south on 13 June 1959. *Gerald Druce/Online Transport Archive*

Class C 0-6-0 No 31714 is seen awaiting departure from Dover Priory. *Fred Ivey/Online Transport Archive*

In 1961 Class Q1 N0 33028 is pictured with a two-coach train at East Farleigh with a westbound service. The signal box and wooden-built station building are both still extant. *Fred Ivey/Online Transport Archive*

Class U1 No 31902 approaches Edenbridge with a Down service on 21 August 1960. *Fred Ivey/Online Transport Archive*

In 1958 Class R1 No 31010 is pictured on duty at Folkestone Harbour station. *Fred Ivey/Online Transport Archive*

On 20 April 1957 'Battle of Britain' No 34086 *219 Squadron* approaches the Up platform at Folkestone Junction with the 10.50am service from Ramsgate to Charing Cross. *Julian Thompson/Online Transport Archive*

During April 1957 'Battle of Britain' No 34090 *Sir Eustace Missenden, Southern Railway* **passes through Folkestone Warren station with a Down service.** *Julian Thompson/Online Transport Archive*

Goudhurst station viewed from the on 10 June 1961 – two days before the station was officially closed; freight facilities were also withdrawn on 12 June 1961. *John Phillips/Online Transport Archive*

Hawkhurst station on 6 May 1961. By this date the branch was approaching its final closure although the station itself still looks in reasonable fettle even if the track is weed-strewn. *John Phillips/Online Transport Archive*

Class O1 No 31065 – later preserved – and an unidentified 'Terrier' 0-6-0 are pictured at Headcorn Junction, northern terminus of the Kent & East Sussex. *Neil Davenport/Online Transport Archive*

High Halden Road station viewed looking towards the north-west on 3 December 1953. *Neil Davenport/Online Transport Archive*
The exterior of Horsmonden station on 26 May 1961. *Gerald Druce/Online Transport Archive*

A pre-grouping view of Lydd station looking towards the north-west with the goods yard and the connection to the Lydd Military Railway on the left. *John Meredith Collection/Online Transport Archive*

Class H 0-4-4T No 31523 takes water in Maidstone West station. *Marcus Eavis/Online Transport Archive*

Class 2H (later Clas 205) DEMU No 1120 stands in the platform at New Romney & Littlestone-on-Sea in March 1964. *Phil Tatt/Online Transport Archive*

Paddock Wood station with push-pull set No 715 towards the end of its life (it was withdrawn in March 1962). *Fred Ivey/Online Transport Archive*

The Down 'Golden Arrow' passes through Penshurst in January 1960 behind 'Battle of Britain' No 34085 *501 Squadron*. *Derek Cross*

The ex-SECR Class O1 No 31065 is seen again, this time in front of the small shed at Rolvenden with the station in the background.
F. E. J. Ward/Online Transport Archive

In May 1951 a virtually brand-new 'Britannia' No 70004 *William Shakespeare* passes through Sandling with the Down 'Goden Arrow'. *Derek Cross*

'Schools' class No 30927 *Clifton* approaches Staplehurst station with a westbound service in 1957. The station originally had staggered platforms – as seen here but the eastbound platform was later relocated westwards. *Fred Ivey/Online Transport Archive*

Tenterden St Michaels Halt was, as can be seen here, a somewhat basic structure. *John L. Smith/Online Transport Archive*

The exterior of Tenterden Town station. *John Meredith Collection/Online Transport Archive*

BR Standard 2-6-4T No 80138 awaits departure from Tonbridge with an Up service. *Fred Ivey/Online Transport Archive*

An Up service formed of set No 620 and an unidentified tender locomotive are pictured departing from Tunbridge Wells Central in 1958. *Fred Ivey/Online Transport Archive*

An unidentified BR Standard 2-6-4T departs eastbound with a service from Tunbridge Wells West on 11 June 1965. *Rev A. M. Logan/Online Transport Archive*

Class H 0-4-4T No 31305 is pictured approaching Wateringbury with an eastbound service. The goods shed in the background is still extant even though freight facilities were withdrawn from the station as long ago as 1961. *Fred Ivey/Online Transport Archive*

A Day in the Life
Photographs by Neil Davenport/Online Transport Archive

Viewed from the south is the three-road shed at Three Bridges with Class E4 No 32520 closest to the camera. The 0-6-2T was to be based at the shed throughout its BR career, being finally withdrawn I January 1957. A total of 70 of the Robert Billinton-designed 'E4s' were constructed at Brighton between December 1897 and September 1903; all passed to BR with the first withdrawals taking place during 1955; the last quartet were withdrawn in early 1963.

On 30 December 1949 Arthur and Neil Davenport visited the sheds at Redhill and Three Bridges. The following views record some of the variety of locomotives and workings that they saw that day.

Opposite top: **Still bearing its SR number, Class C2x No 2447 was not to be renumbered until March 1951. All 45 of the class – nicknamed 'Large Vulcans' – were inherited by BR in 1948; the first of the rebuilt locomotives was modified in 1908 but it was not until 1939 and 1940 that the last examples to be rebuilt were completed. Withdrawals commenced in 1957 with No 32447, allocated to Norwood Junction throughout the BR era, succumbing in early February 1960.**

Bottom: **Recorded with an Up service at Redhill is Class E1 31160; although sporting its BR number, the locomotive retains 'Southern' on its tender. It had been renumbered in January 1949. The first of the 'E' class locomotives to be rebuilt was SECR No 179 in 1919; the following year a further 10 were rebuilt by Beyer, Peacock. All 11 passed to BR but the first withdrawal occurred in 1949 and all were withdrawn by the end of 1961. No 31160, which had been allocated to Stewarts Lane at nationalisation but, when pictured here, was based at Bricklayers Arms, was a relatively early casualty, being withdrawn in February 1951.**

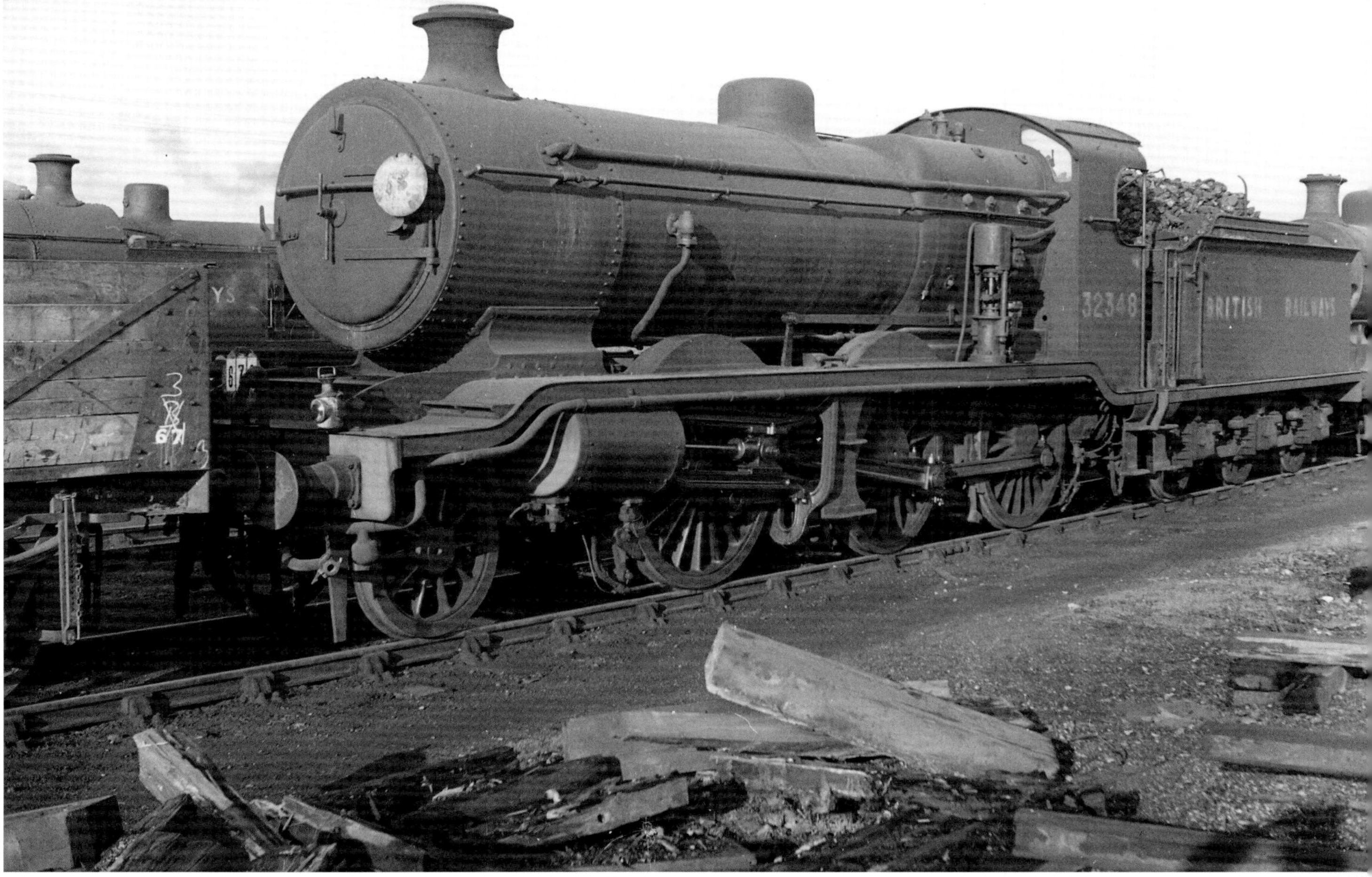
32348
BRITISH RAILWAYS

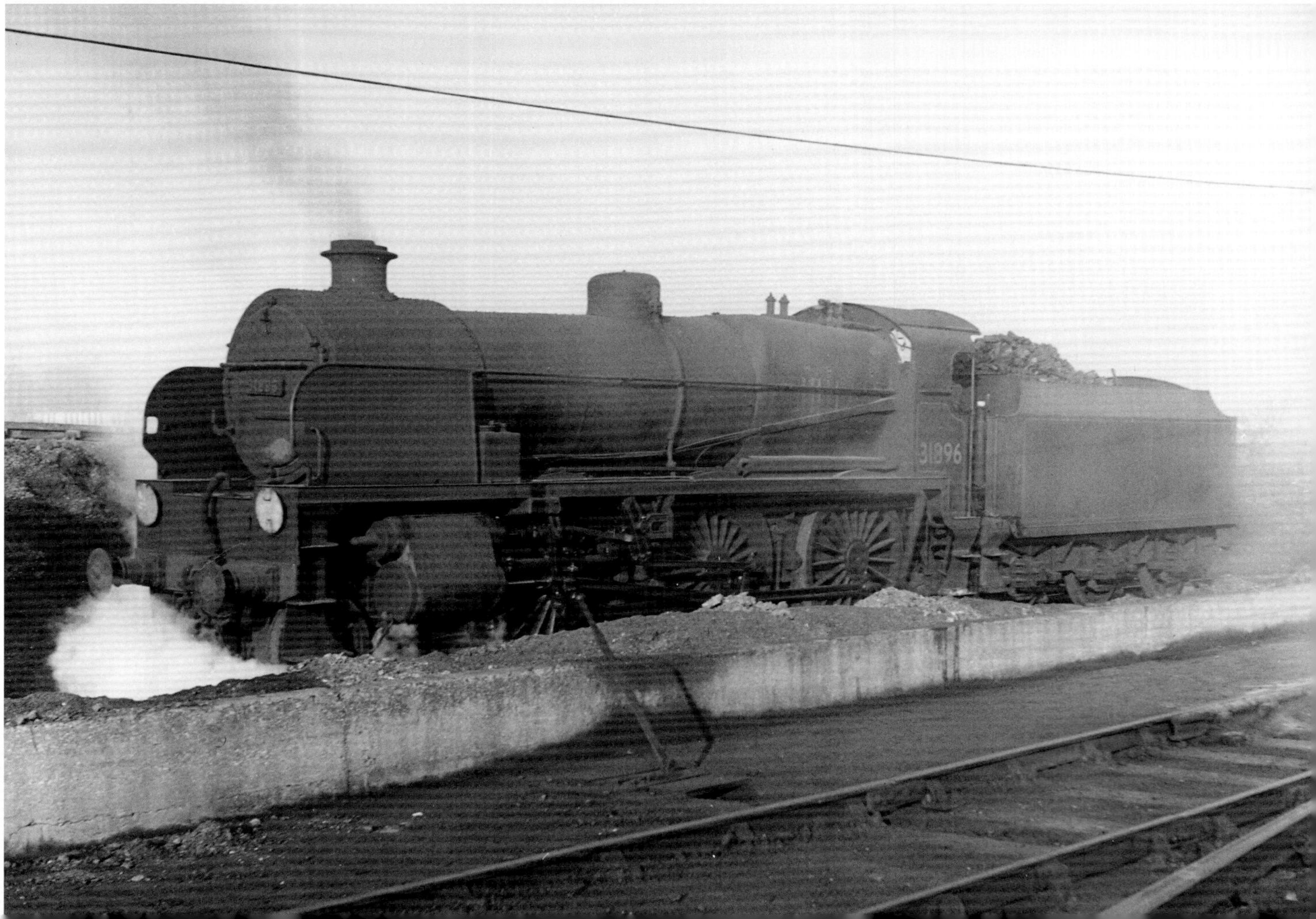
31896

A reminder of the grime associated with steam operation: three locomotives receive attention from the firemen and cleaners at Redhill. This view records the three-road brick-built shed before it underwent rebuilding the following year. This work included the replacement of the original slate roof with an asbestos pitched roof over each track and an asbestos gable at the southern end.

Opposite top: **Designed by Lawson Billinton, a total of 17 of the planned 20 Class K 2-6-0s were completed at Brighton Works between 1913 and 1921. No 32348, which had gained its BR identity in May 1948 (although still lacking its smokebox number plate), was allocated to Eastbourne when recorded here; transferred to Three Bridges in October 1950, the Mogul was to spend the next year being somewhat itinerant, spending brief periods at Brighton, Three Bridges again and Bricklayers Arms, before a final move in the autumn of 1951 saw it return to Three Bridges, where it was to remain for the rest of its operational life. Like all of this successful type, it was withdrawn in late 1962.**

Bottom: **New from Eastleigh Works in March 1931, No 31896, which had gained its BR number in July 1948, was allocated to Redhill when recorded on this visit. Except for a brief four-month sojourn to Brighton in 1951, the locomotive remained at Redhill until May 1955. It then spent time at Stewarts Lane, Tonbridge, Feltham and Norwood Junction before being withdrawn exactly 13 years after it was pictured here on 30 December 1962.**

Reflecting the fact that ex-GWR locomotives operated over the line from Reading to Redhill, one of the large class of 2-6-0s designed by Churchward and introduced in 1911, No 6363, was pictured on Redhill shed during the visit. This locomotive was completed at Swindon Works in April 1925 and, when recorded here, was allocated to Reading, where it was to remain until reallocated to Oxley in January 1951. Between then and September 1964, when it was withdrawn, the Mogul was to be based at no fewer than nine other sheds.

Opposite top: Pictured awaiting departure with a northbound service is Class B4x No 2070. Nominally a rebuild of the Class B4 4-4-0 designed by Lawson Billinton, a total of 12 were converted between August 1922 and January 1924. Eastbourne-allocated No 2070, which had originally been built by Sharp, Stewart & Co in September 1901 and named *Holyrood*, was rebuilt in May 1923. Although all 12 passed to BR, only three survived to be given their BR identity with No 2070 succumbing unrenumbered in August 1951.

Bottom: The second of the trio of the Bulleid/Raworth Co-Co electric 'Booster' locomotives, No 2002, heads southbound with a freight as it passes an unidentifiable 0-6-0. New in 1945, the locomotive had been renumbered in early May 1949. At this stage the locomotive sports an experimental light blue livery (having lost its original malachite green livery in 1948); it was exhibited to the Railway Executive at Addison Road (Kensington) station in this livery. Shortly after it was recorded here, the locomotive was repainted in the new black and aluminium livery adopted by BR for non-steam locomotives.

Index of locations

Corrigenda

With thanks to David Hodge a couple of factual corrections to *Southern Way 72*. On page 20 reference is made to No 34057 *Biggin Hill* being the last remaining unrebuilt Bulleid Pacific. Whilst it was a late survivor, it was not in fact the last in operation. That honour goes to No 341902 *Lapford*. David cites the caption to a photograph by Keith Lawrence in John H. Bird's *Southern Steam*: 'This poignant photograph shows the very last working of an unmodified Bulleid Pacific, No 34102 *Lapford*, passing Weybridge on the 12.38 Waterloo go Basingstoke van train on July 5th 1967. After completing its journey *Lapford* ran light engine to Eastleigh shed to drop its fire for the last time, before being hauled off to Wales and scrapping.' He continues: 'Of course, one must not forget 34023 Blackmore Vale, which was destined for preservation. It would appear from the tables at the end of John Bird's book that she was not employed in the last week of steam on the Southern.' Secondly, on page 62 the description of Groombridge station refers to 'Uxbridge'; this should, of course, have read 'Uckfield'.

On 17 September 2005 No 455824 is seen in Southern livery approaching Clapham Junction with a service for London Bridge via Crystal Palace.
Geoffrey Tribe/Online Transport Archive

The
Southern Way
The regular volume for the Southern devotee
MOST RECENT BACK ISSUES

  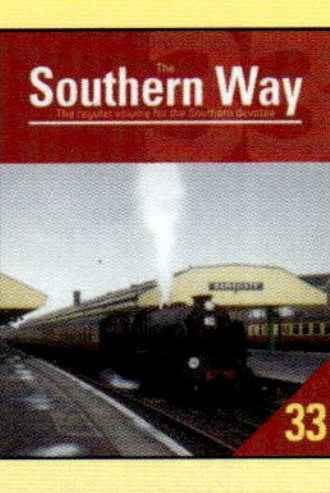    

     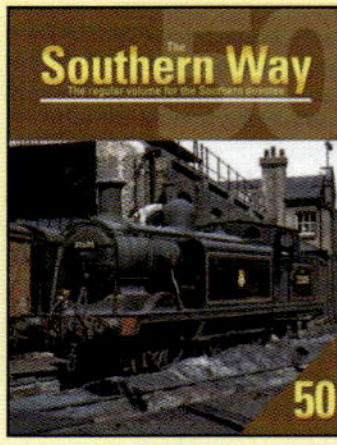 

      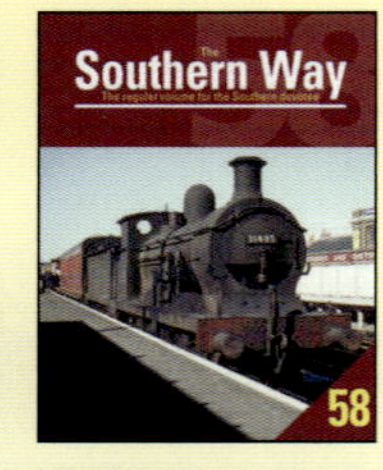

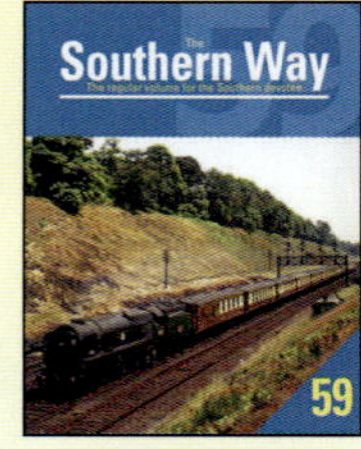   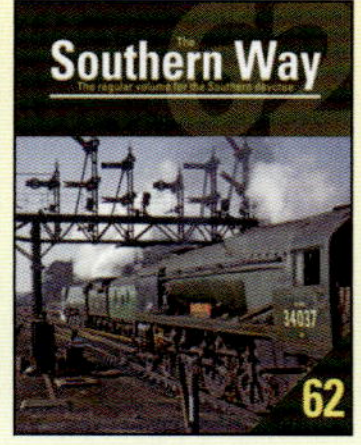  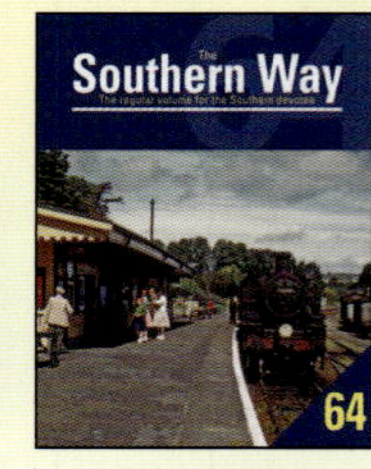 

      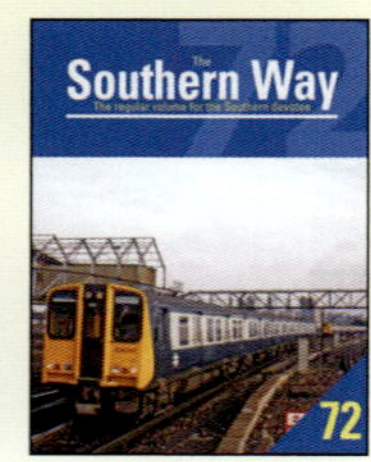

£11.95 each
£12.95 from Issue 7
£14.50 from Issue 21
£14.95 from Issue 35

Subscription for four
issues available
(Post free in the UK)
www.crecy.co.uk

The Southern Way is available from all good book sellers, or in case of difficulty, direct from the publisher. (Post free UK) Each regular issue contains at least 96 pages including colour content.